CAN-DO
REAL ESTATE

CAN-DO
REAL ESTATE

STABLE SUCCESS
FROM THE GROUND UP

ALI JAMAL

ForbesBooks

Published by ForbesBooks, Charleston, South Carolina.
Member of Advantage Media Group.

ForbesBooks is a registered trademark, and the ForbesBooks colophon is a trademark of Forbes Media, LLC.

Printed in the United States of America.

10 9 8 7 6 5 4 3 2 1

ISBN: 978-1-94663-381-1
LCCN: 2020917187

Cover design by Matthew Morse.
Layout design by Wesley Strickland.

This custom publication is intended to provide accurate information and the opinions of the author in regard to the subject matter covered. It is sold with the understanding that the publisher, Advantage|ForbesBooks, is not engaged in rendering legal, financial, or professional services of any kind. If legal advice or other expert assistance is required, the reader is advised to seek the services of a competent professional.

Advantage Media Group is proud to be a part of the Tree Neutral® program. Tree Neutral offsets the number of trees consumed in the production and printing of this book by taking proactive steps such as planting trees in direct proportion to the number of trees used to print books. To learn more about Tree Neutral, please visit **www.treeneutral.com**.

Since 1917, Forbes has remained steadfast in its mission to serve as the defining voice of entrepreneurial capitalism. ForbesBooks, launched in 2016 through a partnership with Advantage Media Group, furthers that aim by helping business and thought leaders bring their stories, passion, and knowledge to the forefront in custom books. Opinions expressed by ForbesBooks authors are their own. To be considered for publication, please visit **www.forbesbooks.com**.

*To my family, who have been my biggest supporters,
my foundation, and my driving force. Thank you for your guidance
and enduring belief in me to fulfill Stablegold Hospitality's mission of
providing affordable housing across the United States.*

CONTENTS

FOREWORD

Throughout history, the business of real estate has proven to be the single most consistent investment for building long-term, sustainable wealth. We've seen proof of this since medieval times, while kings who owned the most land embraced true power. We still see it today when business moguls such as Ray Kroc build vast enterprises like McDonald's for the primary purpose of real estate investing. Despite these indisputable historical patterns, many of us do not know or understand how to profit from this irreplaceable commodity.

The challenge has been that there exists a general assumption that wealth creation through real estate is isolated to arenas controlled by large private companies and/or seemingly larger-than-life business leaders. These seemingly untouchable and beyond-reproach individuals propagate the impression that the ideas and knowledge needed to succeed in real estate are available only to a select few and are not accessible to the common person.

Ali Jamal, in this wonderfully written book, shows us that all of those assumptions are wrong. His own journey illustrates how growing one's own acumen and skills in this field, mixed with hard work and persistence, can prove to be the secret sauce that leads to success and wealth. Despite being one of the smartest people I have had the pleasure of calling a friend, his heart and generosity in regard to sharing his knowledge through stories of his personal growth exemplify how anyone can achieve the knowledge they need to excel in this field and create for themselves incomes that can enhance their personal and professional lives.

The strategies he lays out in a number of eloquent personal stories detail a path for success that can be adopted by anyone. I remind the reader that Ali achieved his success through hard work and a dedication to attaining his goals. His career trajectory is an example of how anyone can succeed at real estate when they take the time and effort to better understand this valuable industry and how to successfully navigate its myriad opportunities and risks. He openly shares that understanding with the reader and goes beyond by allowing the reader to enter some of his darkest moments and see how he overcame them with creative thinking and determination.

Can-Do Real Estate: Stable Success from the Ground Up is not a quick-fix book. It is a story of one person's journey that can be adapted to any of our lives. As you read this book, take the opportunity to relate your journey to his and contemplate how you would have handled those experiences and opportunities differently. Take the time to understand how Ali's journey to the top of his profession started with a simple decision—whether to spend his hard-earned savings on a depreciating asset such as a car or to lay the seed for a real estate portfolio that has made him one of the most respected young businesspeople in the industry.

Rahim Charania
Chairman, Three Ring Studios
CEO, American Fueling Systems

ACKNOWLEDGMENTS

I have to start by thanking my amazing family—first and foremost, my mother. She worked long hours and invested so much time in teaching me about business and, more important, how to be a good person. Without her, I would truly not be where I am today.

My father had the biggest heart of any person I have ever met. He taught me that life is about what you can give back versus what you take.

My uncles—Abbas Ismail, Sadru Ismail, and Pyaruli Ismail—were instrumental in taking a chance and investing in me when most others would not. Over and above that, they have been a source of wisdom, encouragement, and support my entire life. My sisters have also been a support throughout my life. From my eldest sister, Hassina, who babysat me when our mother was trying to make ends meet by working overtime shifts, to my sister Zahra, who beat up bullies for me in elementary school. It has been so rewarding to see them grow into the intelligent, hardworking, kind, and successful women they are today.

My wife, Shaba Jamal, and my daughters, Ava and Lylah Jamal—you are my world. The reason I wake up with a smile on my face and the reason I go to sleep the same way. If everything were lost tomorrow, our family would be all I need to sustain me.

I have also been blessed with some of the best mentors a person could ask for: Craig Williams, Shaun Bradley, Roberta Kelly, Tatsuya Nakagawa, Darlene Gering, and many others. I owe you more than you can imagine.

I would also like to thank our project manager, Rachel Griffin, and our team of editors, including Bonnie Hearn Hill, Zahra Jamal, and Josh Houston, for their help in getting this book to the finish line. The success of the book is in large part due to their care, competence, and ingenuity with the written word.

INTRODUCTION

Buy land. They're not making it anymore.

—Mark Twain

It all started with a car—a sexy, electric-blue, souped-up sports car. More about that later. First, though, I want to tell you why I wrote this book and what I hope it can do for you.

If you've picked up this book because you heard me speak, or if you've read an article about me, you are probably interested in achieving financial freedom through investing in real estate. I can help you with that. In fact, helping and mentoring others to find success in this business I love is one of my greatest passions. However, it's not my only passion. My desire to help those less fortunate has driven me from a young age, and when you learn more about my background, you'll understand why I know what it's like to have little but hope.

I'm excited about this topic, and not only because, in fewer than eight years, I took an empty building and converted it into a privately owned real estate investment firm with 1,500 rental units that produces $9 million in annual sales. I'm also excited because I've developed this portfolio in the affordable housing segment. As I acquired these properties, my company, Stablegold Hospitality, established the Economy

Hotel brand because I had a vision of creating sustainable living for southern Atlanta's low-income population.

I never dreamed the company would reach this level of success, and I had no idea it would pioneer a new business model for the hospitality industry. I call my approach Can-Do Real Estate because it's about taking action, not daydreaming, and not waiting for a future someday that may or may not arrive. It's about moving forward right now—knowing you *can* and then finding a way to *do*.

I learned this at a young age, against my will at first, and then, taking some basic values from my parents, I ran with those values. Throughout this book, I'm going to give you examples of how I dealt with a challenge or faced a problem, and then I'm going to give you my version of a flash card, encapsulating the lessons I want you to remember.

And in case you're wondering—yes, you will have to deal with challenges, and you will encounter problems. As you'll soon learn, if you haven't already experienced it, there's an arc of success. The goal isn't just to weather the storms but to be inspired and excited to weather them. There's no way you can control every aspect, especially when investing, as I do, in affordable housing. The clientele can be very dynamic, and when you're housing three thousand people a day, you'll run into a lot of tidal waves you'll need to ride back to shore. Even in the most challenging situations, you can find your own strength and take courage from your personal mission.

In the pages that follow, I'm going to explore topics like making the first big investment and charting the growth of a company from can-do to success. I learned these lessons the hard way, but now you can learn from me. We'll also take an honest look at finding the right people, emphasizing accountability, providing opportunities to grow, and living by core values and focus. Of course, your path will be different from mine, but if you have the desire and the willingness to work, you *Can Do* in the field of real estate, and you will be able to build your own stable success from the ground up.

In the next chapter, I'm going to show you how I bought my first investment, with all the steps you need to take, right down to ensuring

> ## It matters only that you take that first step, and then another.

you look the part when asking for a loan. I'm also going to share one of the most important lessons my hardworking mother ever taught me. Finally, I'm going to remind you what you probably already know: it doesn't matter where you begin. It matters only that you take that first step, and then another.

CHAPTER 1

WHERE I STARTED, WHAT I LEARNED, AND HOW THAT CAN HELP YOU

Create a vision, and never let the environment, other people's beliefs, or the limits of what has been done in the past shape your decisions.
—Tony Robbins

Now, back to that sports car.

If that doesn't sound like a career motivator to you, remember that I was nineteen years old at the time, and yes, I really had my eye on that electric-blue car. I shared my goal with my mom, who was smart about money and just about everything else.

"You need to save $20,000 for the down payment," she said.

That became my main goal in life. Over the next two years, I worked to save up the money for that car. Finally, I had the money. I was ready.

I went to my mom and told her what I had, and she said the last thing I ever expected to hear.

"No way, Ali!"

"What?" She couldn't be denying me. "We had a deal, Mom. You said you were going to cosign if I made the down payment."

"No way," she said again, as if I hadn't heard her the first time. "I am not going to sign off on you getting that car. It is a depreciating asset."

That's my mom: *depreciating, appreciating, bottom line.* I got that, but she had tricked me, and I was still pretty angry.

"What am I going to buy instead?" I asked.

"You're going to put that money on this condo in downtown Vancouver," she said. "Your dad said we can get one for $170,000."

At this point, I tried calling my mom's brother, Abbas Ismail, in the UK, to convince him this was not a good idea. "You need to support my decision to buy a car instead," I insisted. No luck.

My uncle adamantly disagreed with me, and he had the nerve (and, as it turned out, the good judgment) to side with my mom. From this point on, he continually encouraged me to invest in real estate and became a strong inspiration for me to this day.

Although my parents were divorced by then, they were on good terms, and my dad was living downtown less than a block from this development.

"You've really got to look at getting the kids to invest in this project," he told my mom, referring to my two sisters and me. "It's a great opportunity."

From the time he and my mom first arrived in Canada, he had shown a talent for coming up with brilliant ways to make money. So when he pointed out that potential development, they decided it would be my first investment in life—even though it wasn't a willing one on my part.

We went forward and purchased and then rented out the property, and in 2002, my mom gave me a 1989 Dodge Colt to drive around.

She thought it was a great trade-off. I wasn't so sure at the time. But then, something happened.

Over the next two years, the Vancouver real estate market really skyrocketed, and so did the value of that condo I hadn't wanted to buy. If not for my dad's sharp eye, my mom's good sense, and my uncle's execution, I'd be driving around a rust bucket right now as opposed to having an $800,000 condominium in my investment portfolio.

How Does a Young Person Get a Loan? Very Carefully!

That condo represented a major turn for me in attitude and action. Before I did anything else, though, I needed to get a mortgage—my first one. At age nineteen, I didn't give much thought to how that would happen, but if I had thought about it, I probably would have assumed that I would just walk into the bank, put down my twenty grand, and say, "Lend me some money, will you?"

Fortunately for me, my uncles from London were in town. After the expulsion from Uganda, Uncle Abbas moved to the UK and started a chain of pharmacies. After selling them, he launched a chain of bed-and-breakfasts with his brothers, Sadru and Pierre. Very smart men, my uncles. Right away, they were curious about what I was doing to make sure I got the mortgage loan.

"What's your plan, Ali?" Uncle Abbas asked.

"Well," I replied. "We're going to the bank."

I knew there probably should have been more to my answer, especially when he shook his head and said, "Not quite. Ali, you're going to go and buy a proper suit and wear it to the bank. You aren't just going to show up in your track pants."

"All right," I said, realizing how much I didn't know about this world of real estate and finance.

"Also, you're going to have your sister help you put together a portfolio, which is going to give the bank an idea of how you're going to be able to pay the mortgage every month."

I was stunned but grateful, and I knew he was right. I had $20,000. The condo was selling for $170,000. The gap between what I had and what I wanted to borrow depended on how trustworthy and, yes, mature I appeared. The day arrived, and wearing my new three-piece suit, I entered the bank with Zahra, my uncle, and my mom. The banker was looking at me like, "*What is this?*" Yet he must have been impressed with my uncle, my sister, and my mom, because I got the loan—at age nineteen.

That opened my eyes to how the real world works. Now I understood why my elder sister, Hassina, always looked exceptionally professional before walking into a business meeting, as if preparing to meet the CEO of Gucci.

How you approach people makes a big difference in how they treat you. If you don't look and speak the part, it can be detrimental to your success.

From Bridging Goal to That All-Important Focus

I learned four important lessons from that first experience.

The first is what I think of as a bridging goal. That goal is the first one you see because you don't understand the bigger picture, and that's fine. That's what the car was for me—a primary goal to motivate me to save enough money until I crossed the bridge to the bigger goal: my first real estate purchase. Earlier, I couldn't comprehend the value of the ultimate goal, but I could grasp the importance of saving money for something I (thought) I wanted.

The second was the realization that I actually could save money when I was focused on the prize. Yes, it required hard work and sacrifice, but when I realized I could save that kind of money in two years, the knowledge of my ability to do so empowered me in a way that nothing else could.

The third was that I didn't know enough to be in charge of spending $20,000. I needed the advice of someone older and more experienced.

The fourth lesson was so basic that I shouldn't have had to learn it from my uncle, and you shouldn't have to learn it from me: dress the part.

My Parents' Journey: Laying a Path to My Success

It's easy to focus on only our own lives and our own goals, but if we focus on our parents' journey, we can decide if we want to follow their path—or not. We can also learn a great deal about why they act as they do.

If you've seen the film *The Last King of Scotland*, you might remember that it is about a Scottish doctor who, on a medical mission in Uganda, becomes the personal physician and then confidant of dictator Idi Amin. As the doctor learns about his confidant's barbaric schemes, his goal is to leave Uganda alive. That was my parents' goal as well. In 1972, they were expelled from the country and had forty-eight days to leave. That's it. Forty-eight days to leave the country where my mother worked as a biology teacher and my dad operated a fleet of taxicabs.

In August 1972, Idi Amin accused Uganda's South Asian population of disloyalty, commercial malpractice, and nonintegration, and he gave them—approximately eighty thousand people—ninety days to leave. Finally in the 1980s, after Idi Amin was overthrown, efforts were made to reprocess citizenship applications primarily to entice Asians to come back and restore Uganda after its economic downfall.

More than twenty-seven thousand of these Asians, among them my uncle Abbas, whom I mentioned earlier in this chapter, went to the United Kingdom. Others emigrated to India and Kenya. My parents were among the six thousand who moved to Canada. What they found there, in this new and different environment, was a tightly hinged door.

My dad worked in construction and took whatever odd jobs he could find. My mom's teaching credential wasn't recognized, and at first, she went door to door in our apartment complex, desperately trying to sell homemade naan and roti.

Finally, about three years after they arrived in Canada, she was lucky enough to get a full-time administrative job for the Insurance Corporation of British Columbia. In five or six years, my dad bought a Mac's convenience store, and Mom cosigned on the loan. During a period of economic upheaval, the store didn't succeed. Still, that disappointment did not stop my mom. She continued to work and was very keen on purchasing property. The idea of paying rent on someone else's investment held no appeal for her, and before long, she had an opportunity to buy a house in Vancouver.

However, because she had already cosigned on the Mac's store, the bank was not willing to give her a loan. Her dream of getting her family out of the apartment complex was in danger of failing. Mom talked about her struggles to a family friend.

"I have a contact at the Business Development Bank of Canada," he said. "I might be able to talk them into giving you this mortgage."

She agreed to move forward with the application, and he really helped her get that loan, a rare move for a bank to make. Mom had her house. We had a home.

By the time I arrived, we were a family of six—my mom and dad, my two sisters, my dad's younger brother who had Down syndrome, and me—all sharing one bathroom. From the beginning, I was surrounded, not only by family members but by ambition and motivation, although to me, it was just the way life was.

Building Rental Revenue

Not long after they bought the house, one day while my father was hanging out with his younger brother on the patio, he called Mom over.

"I have an idea," he said. "Why don't we cover up this patio and turn it into a suite?"

She went for the idea, and, with a loan from my mom's sister, Zarina, they converted that little space of our home, which was already the top unit of a duplex, into an actual suite that they rented out. A year later, my mom converted our open garage into another suite. So she had rental revenue from the bottom of the house, from the converted patio, and from the former garage. We were cash flowing, and my mom started to buy more real estate, including our neighbor's house, which she converted into multiple units. In five or six years, she owned thirty units in five houses. She went from bankruptcy to thirty units in that little time. After she and my dad divorced, she was basically a single mother managing those units, working full time, and raising three kids.

Needless to say, she did not throw money around. If I had to come up with one word to describe the way my mom managed her finances, I'd say *militaristically*! She made sure that we lived humbly and below our means. She put money into savings and paying down debt, and she focused on preserving wealth for future generations.

I didn't know we were being frugal. Mom bought everything in bulk, and we might have the same thing for dinner four days in a row. The way we were brought up taught us to appreciate the simplicity of life. It also taught us the value of hard work. Mom was up at five thirty or six o'clock in the morning. She fed us, took us to school, worked all day, picked us up, and was finished by about eight o'clock at night. She did this almost every day for twenty-five years.

Tough times don't have to destroy you.

She was also very religious and spiritual, so while other kids were sleeping, we had to go to mosque with her for morning meditation every day from three to five a.m.

What did I learn from my parents' journey? I learned that tough times don't have to destroy you. I learned the importance of creative thinking, making the most of what you have, and allowing your imagination to think, *What if?* I also learned that regardless of the number of hours in one day, you can choose to fill those hours with everything that is important to you and your future—or you can choose to fill them with nothing. My parents' journey taught me independence. Because of that journey, I felt an eternal connection to them and their legacy of first survival and then financial success.

My First Real Jobs and What They Taught Me

Remember your first job? You were probably still in school and trying to balance your need for cash with the other demands of your young life. These early jobs teach us responsibility and independence, and they prepare us for the real world of work. They also teach us to manage our own money.

Although I worked in those early days, I can't say that I was the best student. Basketball was my passion. When I was growing up, we lived across the street from an elementary school, and a basketball hoop beckoned from just outside our house. I must have spent 80 percent of my childhood at that hoop, and by now, you won't be surprised when I say my mom wasn't extremely excited about that. If I was going to be a jock, she wanted me to be a jock with career opportunities in front of me.

That conflict between Ali the basketball player and Ali the entrepreneur fizzled when it became clear that I wasn't ever going to reach the height necessary to tower over other athletes. I was deflated, even though I played for my senior basketball team and was one of the best players in my school, winning its most valuable player title in grade ten. Still, the inches didn't lie, and I started to realize I wasn't going to be making a career out of professional basketball.

Even though my heart wasn't yet into school, I took courses at Douglas College to get an idea of what I wanted to do as a long-term career. In the meantime, my sister Zahra started working as a bookkeeper for the student paper.

When a sportswriter position opened up, she said, "I know you can do this, Ali."

I had no business being a writer for the student paper and told her so.

"But you'll get a stipend," Zahra insisted. "And you're already on the sports scene. All you have to do is just go to games and write up what happened."

I knew the job required more than that, and to compensate for my lack of ability, I started writing ten articles a week, and not just on college sports. Sports in general, opinion pieces—you name it. I just wrote, and my hard work garnered a little bit of respect from the other writers if not from myself.

Soon, Zahra and others discovered her own talent for writing, and she planned to transfer to an editorial position.

"Would you be interested in taking over my job as a bookkeeper at the paper?" she asked me.

I had no more business being a bookkeeper than I had being a sportswriter, but she vouched for me and said she knew I could do the job.

"Bookkeeping isn't rocket science," she told me. "You can do that and also sell ads."

She then explained that the paper was creating a business manager position. That meant that I could earn not only a salary but a commission. That year, I brought in thousands of dollars in advertising revenue for the school newspaper. That was the greatest sense of achievement I had experienced before I earned the money for the car that became the down payment on my first condo.

But this was community college, and when one or two young people make a lot of money, that raises the eyebrows of the other workers who do not. My income dramatically increased from earning a $200 stipend. Before long, I guessed I had probably run my course, and I began to transition out of that job.

By then, I was eighteen, and I was hired as a courier for Custom House Courtesy Exchange. At the same time, I also started a retail job for HomeSense, an off-price home furnishings chain operated by TJX and similar to TJ Maxx.

My first paycheck went to my mom. By the age of seventeen, I was paying rent to her. Something had changed, though. I had discovered the difference between getting a paycheck and creating money for yourself by building relationships. When you work for someone else, that someone else is controlling your paycheck, I realized. As an entrepreneur, only you create your paycheck.

Selling advertising was a lot easier and more profitable than putting in retail hours or slaving at the computer, trying to write articles about sports. My experiences taught me the value of using my human capital. As I soon learned, the entrepreneurial spirit is strong in the United States. The more I started leaning toward that entrepreneurial approach, the more seriously I considered relocating to take advantage of growth opportunities.

In a 2013 article for *Forbes*, serial entrepreneur Kevin Ready wrote, "Get out at Enough, and move on to the projects that have life-defining meaning, even if that means leaving money on the table."[1]

I wrote this book to teach you—regardless of your age—how to use my Can-Do approach to real estate, but making a lot of money isn't everything. It's just another goal on your checklist.

Regardless of how little your cash flow and how large your dreams, you need to have intentions and a sense of purpose. As a young man, I listened to many positive speakers and motivators. From then on, what drove me was helping others and having a portfolio of properties. Owning land gives you a whole new sense of financial viability, something my mom figured out long before I did. Sure, owning property was also a nice ego stroke, and it felt good. The second thing

---

1   Kevin Ready, "Beyond Profit: The Ultimate Goal of Entrepreneurship," Forbes.com, April 15, 2013.

that was really important was making my family's life a little easier. My mom had worked so hard for as long as I could remember, and part of my driving force was putting her in a position where she could live with a little less pressure and a lot more peace of mind. That was and still is really important to me.

Every year, I look at what we have acquired and where I can potentially take that. As the company has grown, our goals continue to be providing affordable accommodations for those in need. I always had those intentions, and even from a young age, I donated to such causes. Now I'm proud to be able to carry out that early vision. For some entrepreneurs, it's all about making your life great and not worrying about anything else around you. That won't bring you much satisfaction. My intention is about making life better for the people around me.

What about You?

What is your dream? Can you put it in a sentence?

What is your driving force? For me, it was helping others, both those who couldn't find affordable accommodations and my own family, especially my mom. And yes, there was that matter of the car.

Are you willing to plant those seeds that will eventually harvest over time? A major component of those seeds is hard work. Another component—one you need to understand at the outset—is the understanding that there's never any end game. You have to learn how to love the trials and rewards of building a portfolio. When a challenge comes up, you have to have the mindset of enjoying the challenge instead of crying over it. You're going to experience economic downturns and major security breaches, as I have, but the mental shift has to be there. When you can train your mind to make those shifts, you are ahead of most of your competitors, many of whom want to point fingers at someone else or at themselves.

Now I actually love it when problems come up. They give me an opportunity to sharpen my skills. Until we really think about these matters, our first reaction to every problem is panic. That's certainly what happened with the COVID-19 pandemic. In the blink of an eye, the world changed. When something unexpected strikes, the first

> We've had world wars, recessions, and now a major pandemic. But no situation lasts forever.

thing you need to do is lead with calmness and a positive attitude.

Whenever an external event seems out of your control, it's a reminder to look at history. We've had world wars, recessions, and now a major pandemic. But no situation lasts forever. Despite the pain, there is light at the end of the tunnel. You can look at such a situation as one that might put you into bankruptcy, or you can look at it as an opportunity to learn, to grow, to shift your business, and to come out stronger than you ever did before

With that said, I have trained myself—and you can train yourself too—in the midst of any problem, to ask in a calm and rational manner: What does this problem mean? And what is the best way to overcome it? I can pretty much handle most issues now, and by the time you finish this book, so will you.

Lessons Learned

Here's what I learned before and just after I made my first real estate deal at eighteen:

- Follow your bridging goal. That goal is the first you see because you don't understand the bigger picture.

- Know that you can save money when you focus on the prize.

- Seek out the advice of someone older and more experienced.

- Dress the part.

- Tough times don't have to destroy you.

- Creative thinking can make you rich.

- Ask yourself, *What if?*

- Choose to fill the hours of your day with thoughts about everything that is important to you and your future.

- Use your human capital.

- Oh, yes. And don't worry about the car. That or a better one will come later—if you still want it.

In the next chapter, I'm going to describe the career path that led me to my first big purchase.

CHAPTER 2

FROM CONDO TO CAREER

I have nothing in common with lazy people who blame others for their lack of success. Great things come from hard work and perseverance.

—Kobe Bryant

Purchasing the condo turned out to be pretty exciting after all. I later heard the quote attributed to Wayne Dyer, "Go the extra mile. It's never crowded." I already felt that instinctively. I wanted to and was determined to go the extra mile, even though I wouldn't be getting there in that sexy blue car.

Once we finished the condo purchase, I went back to working my two jobs, writing for the college newspaper and working for Custom House Global Foreign Exchange, which is now part of Western Union. During that time, my role was to take currency transfers to various customers across Vancouver. I also hoped to explore other career opportunities because I had some big dreams. The banking world had opportunities for upward mobility. True, I didn't have the background, but as I visited the various branches, I collected business cards—probably close to sixty of them.

I also faxed out my résumé. Let's just say not everyone was thrilled at the prospect of hiring me, this inexperienced kid. Still, one small branch in Vancouver called me back. The woman who did was honest, when we spoke, about my abilities versus their needs.

"We've lost five people," she said.

That was fine with me. The numbers game had worked in my favor—another lesson learned. Sometimes the numbers are against you, but many times, they are not. The only way to know is to get out there and make many connections.

My new job at the North Shore Credit Union was only ten minutes away from my mom's job, and let me tell you, she was so proud that I got to wear a tie to work. Roberta Kelly, my mom's wonderful boss, had been a longtime mentor to her, and I can only guess my mom bragged about me to her all the time. I had grown up around Roberta and knew she respected my mom, Parin, a single mother of three kids, and the fact that she was working so hard to create a future for her family.

I worked at the credit union for about one year and had broken the sales record for getting the most people to sign up for our version of a 401(k). Then Roberta was hired at the Burnaby Chamber of Commerce. She called my mom.

"Parin," she said, "I have a perfect job for your son."

This job would be manager of membership sales for the Burnaby Board of Trade, at three or four times the salary I was currently making.

Over My Head, Proving My Worth

I'm sure I don't have to point out that this was way over my head in terms of qualifications. Still, Roberta had worked as a campaign manager for one of the province's political leaders. With equal dedication, she took on the job of getting me hired.

"This kid has to work for us," she told her colleagues at the chamber.

She put her name on the line for me—something for which I will always be grateful. I went for the interview with the chair, Ed Jaskula, who sat on the board of directors, and he spoke with me about the position. I'm sure he could see that I was super enthusiastic about the job. As the interview progressed, I was certain I was doing well—until the focus of the interview switched to sales and how to develop business.

Then Ed started to ask questions about local politics, such as, "How would you develop relationships with city councillors?"

I just started making up answers on the spot.

Roberta called me the next day and told me the truth.

"They think you have a lot of enthusiasm," she said. "They also think you're super green." I waited, wondering if she would say I had lost the job. Instead, she said, "I told them you have to work for us, or I'm going to leave."

"Thank you," I managed.

"That's right. I told them, 'Either you hire this kid, or I don't want to be here anymore. I believe in him that much.'"

She was like that if she believed in you. This was a woman who still sent out handwritten cards in glitter pen, a woman who was respected by just about everyone. They did not want to lose her. I was twenty-two years old, and the year before, I didn't know how to tie a tie. Thanks to Roberta's belief in me, I learned in a hurry.

The opportunity was pretty amazing, and I'm the first one to raise my hand and say I was carried to that opportunity. My family was ecstatic.

When someone puts their job on the line for you, you don't go in half-assed. I would be in the office at six o'clock in the morning, working until seven o'clock or later at night. I was running on the fuel of their belief in me. It was a pretty potent fuel.

That's key, I think, to taking on any challenge, personal or professional, and conquering it. Just get up, put on your suit, and get to work. You'll come out of it a better person at the end of the day.

As I write this book in early 2020, our business has had some challenges that are the norm in this industry. I wake up earlier, get to work earlier, and hit the road. It's all you can do whether you're running a business or working for an organization. There's no substitute for hard work. You've got to keep pushing, because once you solve one problem, another one is going to pop up. If you haven't dealt with the first one, how are you going to deal with both?

So here I was at my new job, and it was time to roll up my sleeves. I felt there were a lot of eyes on me, and I didn't want to fail the people who believed in me. I didn't know what I was doing—going out selling memberships to small and large business owners who understood business—and here I was coming from a job as a bank teller. At first, I went in with a canned speech, super nervous—and, to be honest, a lot of times I made a fool of myself. Sometimes people hung up on me. Sometimes I had doors slammed in my face. I had a big learning curve, and that's how I looked at it: as a learning curve.

I promised myself I was going to be the best I could be, but it wasn't easy. I pushed through it, and during the first two months, I was making one hundred calls a day. I would call, and if I hit voice mail, I'd hang up and call again. My philosophy was this: even if I had a weak sales pitch, one of these people would want to buy a membership from me. The ratio got better as time went on. The first two months, I sold very few but had a lot in the pipeline. In month three, I had twenty! All the seeds I'd planted started coming up out of nowhere.

Well, I thought. *If I pulled twenty memberships making one hundred calls a day, all I have to do is double my calls.* The harder you work, the higher the numbers. You can apply that to anything. That's basically what we did. When I started, the chamber had two hundred members. In three years, we brought in about one thousand. Yes, my numerous cold calls helped. Equally important, however, I learned to listen.

Over time, as I talked to more businesses, I got a better idea of what was important to them. A canned speech doesn't mean much if you're talking about benefits that aren't important to them. Sales is about asking questions. So, instead of the canned speech, I'd say, "Tell me about your business. What are your challenges?" And guess what? They would tell me. Soon, the process was less about me babbling and more about me listening. It was about coming up with a solution for the company.

I could walk into a meeting and say, "I don't know if your company is the right fit for us. If you think I have the right solution, by all means, I'd love for you to join us."

That completely changes the whole dynamic. Sales for me was really not about talking but listening. It was problem solving.

Three years later, I had developed a track record of success. I was meeting new companies every day. Now companies were actually pursuing me. I got a call from Canadian Manufacturers & Exporters, one of Canada's largest lobby groups. Almost 150 years old, the organization worked for and with 2,500 leading manufacturers from coast to coast. They were hiring a new director of business development in their British Columbia division, and Craig Williams, the previous director, had heard about me through the grapevine and knew I had a reputation for developing memberships. He was entering retirement and wanted to give back to manufacturing communities.

"I've heard you're great and would love to sit down with you," he said. The feeling was mutual.

The scope of this job was larger than just being in Burnaby. He asked me how I would develop the membership for his organization, and this time, I had plenty of ideas. He had a wealth of experience, including thirty to forty years of CEO experience, and seemed like a great leader. *This is a guy I could learn from*, I thought.

The interview went extremely well. He sent me an assessment—and then he sent me a job offer. Around that time, he called me.

"I contacted one of your references, and she talked for an hour and a half, telling me how great you are," he said. "I thought to myself, *I'm just going to give this guy the job*." The reference was my friend and supporter Roberta Kelly, of course.

Looking ahead, I could see myself growing into the CEO position of the organization in the next fifteen years. At the same time, I continued investing in real estate on the side, enjoying the challenges of entrepreneurship.

At this juncture, I had gone to Darlene Gering, the executive director of the Board of Trade, to explain the situation, and she did not want me to leave. We had excellent teamwork, and she felt my departure would leave a void at the office. Yet, she also knew I had to take the next step on my career path, and we parted as friends.

Going Back to the Fundamentals

I had learned from my previous job that if I called one hundred people a day, I would get one or two sales a day. I made a list and started calling companies and setting up meetings for appointments.

Think of basketball players. Even though they've been playing basketball all their lives at the elite level, what do they do when they go to practice? They practice dribbling; they go back to the fundamentals. In this new job, the fundamentals still remained the same. A membership is a membership is a membership. A business is a business is a business. By this time, I was selling to five or six people a day, and I could speak a little more intelligently.

My first week on the job, they didn't have an office ready for me, so I worked out of a boardroom. "If you can give me a phone and a notepad, I'm good," I told them.

Craig, my boss at the time, said, "Your work ethic is unbelievable."

Over the first year, we pretty much doubled the membership, and I was promoted to director of business development and sales for Western Canada.

After a couple of years, I developed a good relationship with Jayson Myers, head of the organization, and was able to travel all over Ontario. I didn't realize how vast and beautiful Canada is. For a young person willing to work hard, this was an amazing job.

Creating Money—and Cash Flow

During this time, I was still investing in real estate and renting out my purchases. I bought an eight-bedroom home up the road from where my mom and I lived and started renting it out to college kids for $500 a month each. After paying down my mortgage, I was earning $1,500 to $2,000 per month. That was a hands-on lesson in how lucrative real estate could be.

If you create enough money, you create cash flow, and cash flow is really cool. *Forget these one- or two-unit buildings*, I thought. Those with a larger number of units created more cash flow. These rooms we were renting out became like microhotels. It's not really surprising that my investing path was leading me to just that—hotels. After all, I had started watching my parents expand our house, and I soon learned it made good sense to invest in more units.

Not long after, our accountant sent me a referral to an investment opportunity in Atlanta, Georgia—a hotel in foreclosure, selling for $1.2 million. Within forty-eight hours of the conversation, I flew out to Atlanta to visit the property. The next day I met with the broker and took a tour of the hotel. After that, I visited the Studio 6 hotel next door. From the front desk clerk, I learned that it was sitting at 100 percent occupancy. I checked the parking lot to confirm it was full. Perfect.

I knew that if we could simply compete with Studio 6 on the price of rooms, we would be in business right away. We just needed to ensure we offered the same product—that is, extended-stay accommodation.

My mental checklist went something like this:

- Good location. Check.

- Decent condition. Check.

- Neighbors next door at Studio 6 running a great occupancy. Check.

We should be able to make it work.

The next day, after gathering all the facts and developing my business case, I called my uncle in London with my referral. I explained that the price was excellent for a concrete building and that the 127-room hotel had once been a Hampton Inn. In return for a cash investment to purchase the facility, I was willing to do all the donkey-work to get it up and running.

He asked me if I was sure about this venture, because he was seventy-plus years old and wouldn't be able to help me operate the property. I would be on my own.

I insisted that I was capable and ready for the challenge.

Miraculously, my uncle had faith in me. So much so that he made an expensive bet on me, even though I had never run a hotel before. At the beginning of my career, I was grateful when Roberta, my mom's friend, put her job on the line to go to bat for me. Now I was humbled—and excited—beyond belief.

Lessons Learned

- There is no substitute for hard work. You've got to keep pushing. The harder you work, the better you'll do.

- The secret to sales is asking questions.

- The fundamentals remain the same.

- When someone believes in you, do your due diligence, and then do whatever it takes to prove them right.

In the next chapter, we'll explore the beginnings of how we created the model that serves our residents and our investors so well today.

CHAPTER 3

BIRTH OF THE MODEL

Business has only two functions: marketing and innovation.
—Peter Drucker

So here I was, feeling a great commitment to my family and myself. I was also excited that I had this opportunity at such a young age. My uncle, who was about seventy-two at the time, flew in from London to work alongside me, and it was pretty much going to be only the two of us at first. We were both exhausted, so we decided to book a room at the Studio 6 next door. On that first night, we did our thought processing and preplanning about how to get our new acquisition up and running.

My uncle is not someone who wants to sit around, taking it easy.

"Look," he said. "Let's go take a tour of the hotel and go through each and every room and, with a pen and a notepad, write down what needs to be done in every single room in the hotel."

"Tonight?" I was jet lagged. "I'm going to sleep."

"No," he insisted. "Let's walk it. We're going to go walk all these rooms with a notebook, and we've got to know everything that's going on in every one of them."

I knew he was right. "Okay," I said. "Let's do that."

As I mentioned before, when I went to see the property initially, I was with the real estate agent, and I had done only a general overview. Although I had studied the hotel from a high-level perspective, my uncle wanted to examine the nuts and bolts. And so we did.

We walked in that first night, into a hotel that had been shut down for two years, a hotel the owners hadn't kept in the best condition but a hotel we now owned. That night, we walked all 127 rooms—and remember, this was in Atlanta, Georgia, in the summertime.

The hotel didn't have working air-conditioning, so there we were—my uncle and me—in our pajamas, late at night, walking through every room of this pretty much neglected building. In each room, my anxiety increased, and not just because I was sweating in that oppressive heat. The more rooms we visited and the more detailed notes I took, the more I started to realize there was a lot more work in each and every one of these rooms than I might have initially anticipated.

> *Damn, did I realize how much work was going to go into this?* I thought. *Did I think through everything? Was I just overambitious?*

As we went through them, my uncle didn't say anything, but I was reminding myself that he was one of my biggest investors, as well as someone who was there to help me. As we got through the last room, I started really questioning myself.

Damn, did I realize how much work was going to go into this? I thought. *Did I think through everything? Was I just overambitious?*

I had all these thoughts going through my head, including the fact that I'd just given up my job. Everything had happened very quickly.

Still, my uncle didn't say anything, and we returned to the Studio 6, where we would spend the night.

He went into his room.

I went into my room.

Thirty minutes later, I heard *knock, knock, knock* at my door, and there he was, holding his notepad.

"I want to talk to you," he said.

"Okay," I told him. This was going to be a long night.

He sat down at the table and asked, "How do you feel about all the rooms that we just saw?"

"You know," I told him, "I didn't realize there was just so much work that needs to be done. We have all these renovations, and we have to make sure every room gets painted. We're going to patch up this and patch up that. It's going to be a pretty daunting task."

He looked at me and shook his head. "You're overthinking this," he said, "getting overly anxious."

Then he asked me to realize a few important things.

"Number one, we have a hotel now that we don't have any mortgage on. We're not accountable to anyone."

"Right," I said.

"And number two, because of that, we can charge the price for rooms that we want to charge, and if we charge the right price for them, there is no way for it to go other than be successful."

"Yes," I said. Although I was still trying to wrap my head around all this, I sensed the wisdom of his words.

"It's going to be successful because the one basic need that everyone has is for accommodation," he told me. "If you can provide that in an affordable fashion, you are going to be golden."

I already knew he was right, and that was a turning point for me because I was at a crossroads where I could have lost my confidence regarding this investment.

"Don't be dejected," he told me. "Don't beat yourself up about it. It's going to be fine. We're just going to have to figure out how we get some of this work done, and then we'll move it forward."

His words carried a lot of weight, so when he said that, I had a boost of confidence and told him, "Yeah, okay, we can do this." I was saying it to myself as well as to him.

"Another thing, before we close up for the rest of the evening," he added. "We're staying at the Studio 6 tonight, but we have our own hotel across the street. We're staying there tomorrow."

"But the hotel is …" I said, trying to make sense of his words. "I mean, it's not functioning, and there's no air-conditioning."

"I really don't care." He shrugged. "That's our hotel, and that's where we're sleeping tomorrow. Period."

That was it. That was the end of that conversation, and so we packed up our luggage in the morning, and that's when I started staying in the hotel.

Up and Running

When we got there that morning, my uncle said, "Pick any room in the hotel that you'd like, and that's going to be your home for the next little while."

I picked the room that was closest to the front desk area because once we had it up and running, I knew I would be needed there. My uncle picked the room right next to mine.

We started the first day with our list of all the things we had to get done. Next, we needed to figure out how we were going to get it done and how we were going to hire people, because we didn't know anyone in Atlanta. We didn't have any major contacts to be able to develop a construction crew. That's where we were at day one. That is where we started.

I had a level of confidence now, though, that we could make it work. My biggest concern was that this was a family investment. People I love were counting on me to make this work. If it was a screwup, we weren't looking at screwing up something small. We were looking at screwing up millions of dollars' worth of real estate. Still, the talk my uncle and I had that first night really got my back straightened up, and I was ready to take on the challenge.

The next day, we needed to look for someone to help us put together a construction crew, someone who had local connections. The broker who had sold us the property was originally from London and had moved to West Palm Beach. In London, he had grown up with a childhood friend, Pete, who had moved to Atlanta. Here's the best part.

"Hey," my broker said. "My good friend Pete owns and operates a whole bunch of hotels there. You should reach out to him, and you guys should connect. Maybe he can help you get your hotel up and running and guide you through the process."

"Awesome," I said, unable to believe this turn of good luck. I called Pete, and he came out to the hotel and said, "Let's grab lunch."

By then, I was twenty-eight, and he was a little older than me. Even at that first lunch, we were like childhood friends ourselves, hanging out like buddies, having a great time. We also shared some good laughs and learned about each other's backgrounds. We got along.

I told him the truth. "You know, I really need someone to help us get this hotel up and running, and I have no idea where to start. My uncle is here, but we still need more help. We have a big box we're converting to an actual hotel operation, and I think I need some guidance."

"No problem," he said. "I'll definitely jump on as a consultant and help you out with construction workers and anything else you need to get the hotel up and running."

"Awesome." I couldn't believe my ears. "That's great."

"I'll walk you through everything," he said. "I can start in the next couple days."

I didn't think it could get any better, but then he asked how I planned to get around.

"I haven't really thought about it," I said.

"You're going to need a truck, especially when you're getting your hotel up and running," he told me. "And if you're doing renovations, your contractors are going to need supplies. You're not going to want them to go picking up supplies on your time. You're going to want to pick up all the materials for them and bring them to the hotel, so they're not wasting any time and are continuing to work."

I could see his point. We definitely needed a truck to save ourselves time and money. He asked if we had access to one, and I admitted that we didn't have one at the moment but could probably get one.

Then, just like that, he motioned to his own truck and said, "You can have this for the next few months. Just give it back to me when you can."

Pete was another angel in my life at the time. He not only gave me his truck, but he opened his household to me, and he was a major reason I survived my first couple of years in Atlanta when otherwise I would have been alone.

After the first six months, my uncle had to return to London. Even though he came back to help me every six or seven months, I was, in essence, there alone. Pete was really a lifeline support for me. He invited me to his home for dinners. He visited me at the hotel almost every day. He provided me with a social circle I would not have had.

Within the next couple of days after giving me his truck, he had set up construction and housekeeping crews for us, and they came into the hotel and started doing all the work, checking off those items on the list my uncle and I had put together.

Not only had Pete helped us accomplish all this, but he had given us one of his key employees.

"You're going to need someone to kind of be your right hand to get things started," he said.

I knew what he meant. We needed someone from the South, and because we were from Vancouver, Canada, we would not have met too many people like that on our own.

> Pricing was going to be key, and we decided to go low, because as my uncle had pointed out, we owned it. We could charge whatever we liked.

Enter Barry. He was the typical stereotype of someone from the South, a really good person, very kind, and the embodiment of southern hospitality. He was initially given to us as a maintenance worker, and he was so great that we used him in every component of the hotel. So he was our front desk agent. He was our maintenance guy. He was our housekeeper when we needed him to be. He was our security team. Barry was absolutely everything to us, an incredible gift.

Thanks to all these opportunities, after about three months, we were finally able to get our occupancy license from the county to open the hotel.

Pricing was going to be key, and we decided to go low, because as my uncle had pointed out, we owned it. We could charge whatever we liked. "Let's start selling rooms, and let's do something that no one else is doing," he said. "And if this undervalues our brand or whatever, who cares? Let's just try to get business in the door right now and start paying some bills. Let's sell all rooms for $25 a night as a marketing tactic and see what happens." The other hotel was selling their rooms for about $50 to $60 dollars a night, so we had basically cut their price point in half, and they were right across the street.

Finally, opening day arrived. I ran the front desk, opening up around six o'clock that morning. Although the first two days were a little slow, we felt like we had some good traction, and then business started picking up. Within the week, half the hotel was full, and what my uncle had predicted was proving to be true—if we priced the rooms right, the market would always be there. By the middle of the next week, we were pretty much at 90 percent occupancy.

We had the ability to do this because we didn't have that huge amount of financial leverage, and so our operating costs were lower than they might have been. I was running the front desk. My uncle was in charge of operations. I had Barry as an all-around employee, and we had one or two housekeepers, so our staffing level was very low, and our operating costs were minimal.

Now, if you multiply $25 times 127 rooms, that's about $3,000 a day, and our outlay in terms of expenses was not that much because, once again, we were controlling our operating costs very aggressively. As a result, we were probably making a profit of at least $1,800 a day. So we were in a business that was cash flowing from day one.

The Business Model

The beauty of this business model is that you get the same consistency of business as you would in a multifamily apartment complex. However, you don't have to go through the lease process and eviction process. Although we try our best to work with individuals and their budgets, we are not left with people staying in the hotel without paying rent for three or four months the way we could be in a multifamily complex. Basically, if they don't pay, the police will evict them from the property right away.

Originally, I wanted to follow a business model similar to Studio 6, an offshoot of Motel 6 that operates extended-stay hotels. I had done some research on how we could operate these types of hotels because I realized very quickly that we needed to go for an affordable hotel brand. A customer on vacation or business travel would not come to this type of hotel. It was too old, and it just did not fit the parameters of what they're looking for.

On the other hand, in this business you are building brand equity in a sense because these people are staying with you for longer periods of time, and you're pulling them in with that price. And once that price point is pulled, once someone is paying $25 a night, it's pretty hard to get them to go to another place and pay $50 or $60, even if that place is that much nicer. If you are working from paycheck to paycheck, if you're working at the Waffle House and getting paid maybe $40 a day, every dollar counts, and $25 a night might just fit right into your budget because you can use that extra $15 for other necessities.

That's what I realized about our business model and our potential customer when we first started. We could offer those potential customers what they needed most, and that was affordability.

The Human Connection

Thirty days later, after our expenses, we were ahead by $35,000 or $40,000, and we were kind of looking at each other like, *Wow, I think we've hit something here.* I had been working for those first thirty days—every day—on that front desk, and what I didn't realize at the time, because I was too distracted by too many other matters, is the fact that I was interacting with each and every guest.

Everyone who paid came down and talked to me about how they felt about the rooms. But the condition of the rooms wasn't what they were interested in. This was a C class asset, an older building that had been shut down for two years. It wasn't the Ritz-Carlton, and I never would say that it was. However, these people were not complaining. They were more focused on talking about their life issues.

They wanted someone at that front desk to listen to what was going on in their lives, and typically it was about financial issues. They also discussed social issues, what challenges they were facing in their lives. As I listened to them and got to know their issues, I gained a deep understanding of what was important to our customer base.

I knew we could adjust our business model based on a lot of that information. I began to understand what some of the struggles were for the people who were staying with us in that affordable housing segment.

One woman told me about her husband who had cancer. Another was an alcoholic and talked about how she became one. Still another was beaten by her boyfriend, and yet another had left Alabama because she was being abused by her father and needed to run away from home. I came across story after story after story, and I started to realize, in a way I hadn't previously, why people were staying at this property for the most affordable price they could find. There was always a story behind it, and it wasn't just that they were trying to save money. Yes, this was the only place they could afford, but there was a reason it was the only place they could afford.

Knowing that, we had to figure out how we could provide services that had value for them. That got that whole thought process going and gave me a little bit more context regarding how we could be more of a support to the community.

My life had changed drastically. I'd left a six-figure job to start a hotel from ground zero,

> In times like that, you've got to have a vision that is stronger than your current discomfort.

living in that hotel, taking no salary and only a stipend for food, going from a sports car to a 1980 Dodge Ram. It was a very big change in lifestyle in a very short amount of time. In times like that, you've got to have a vision that is stronger than your current discomfort. The vision I had then was where I am today—living my life from a financial standpoint on my own terms, not having to answer to anyone other than my investors, my family, and the people who believe in me. Doing something with purpose is part of that vision.

As I interacted with the residents at the front desk, my paradigm shifted. I realized people who need affordable accommodation are just like you and me. I thought, *If we had ten or fifteen or one hundred hotels, think about how much of a dent we could make in homelessness.* Today, we have people who have been living with us for five or six years.

It's a humbling experience when guests are counting out all the money they have, and we can say, "Just give me what you can. We don't want you to go back out there and be without a bed tonight."

I realized that when my parents came to Canada, they might have had similar experiences to what these people were going through, and I knew my story would be very different if I hadn't had my strong support network. Maybe these people didn't have that. When you look at the people factor, it shapes your view of the world and your business. In this demographic, we have two great things going for us. One, we can fill our hotels, and two, we're doing something that falls in line with our ethical code and what we believe.

I believe that code rubs off on our employees and others with whom we deal. Numerous studies suggest that strong ethics lead to employee productivity and retention as well as long-term profitability. A 2019 ethics and compliance study by LRN found that encouraging a corporate conscience among staff made employees more likely to speak out and resulted in increased engagement and stronger ethical decision-making.[2]

One last thing that was really cool for me to see in that first month is what I came to think of as the happiness quotient of our residents. As the hotel filled up, I noticed that the happiness quotient of a lot of the people who were staying with us started to increase. When they came in the first day, all they wanted was to pay their $25 and get a room. They were mad at life. But a week or two later, they seemed happier and more relaxed. I could say it was because they were saving some money by staying with us, but I don't think that was the case. I think what happened and what I saw was more complex than that. There was a sense of community building at that hotel.

People from different parts of life who had gone through different life crises were now hanging out together. They were talking together, they were having a smoke outside together, and they were building that sense of togetherness that wasn't there before.

I started seeing people who had once been strangers babysitting each other's children and treating each other like neighbors. I'm sure not everyone was doing great stuff, but in a broad overview, there was a

---

2   LRN, *Ethics & Compliance Program Effective-
ness Report*, 2019, 6, https://content.lrn.com/
research-insights/2019-ec-program-effectiveness-report.

sense of community being embraced in this hotel, and I don't think in any other type of hotel you would have that interaction among guests.

Typically, if someone is staying at the Marriott, they are going to go to their room with their spouse; they are going to tour the city, find some places to eat out; and they are going to leave in the next couple of days. This was a completely different kind of atmosphere. It wasn't just a bunch of rooms; it was a community. The average person stayed at least three months. The longer I worked the front desk and got to know these people, the more I understood firsthand the importance of building a community and the profound effect that can have on people's happiness. As far back as 1979, Lisa Berkman, director of the Harvard Center for Population and Development Studies, coauthored a seminal study of nearly seven thousand adults in Alameda County, California.[3] "Participants who reported fewer social ties at the beginning of the survey were more than twice as likely to die over the nine-year follow-up period, an effect unrelated to behaviors such as smoking, drinking, and physical activity. Social ties included marriage, contact with friends and relatives, organizational, and church membership."

Other studies on longevity have shown the connection between a support network and longer life. Many of the individuals I got to know as I worked at the front desk didn't have that before they came to the hotel. They may or may not have had family members, but because they didn't have a permanent place to live, they lacked that all-important sense of communal family.

---

3   "The Biology of Emotion—and What It May Teach Us about Helping People to Live Longer," Happiness & Health, Harvard School of Public Health, Winter 2011, https://www.hsph.harvard.edu/news/magazine/happiness-stress-heart-disease/.

Connected to that, I also noticed that these people exhibited less negative judgment toward each other because a lot of the other people staying at the hotel were from similar backgrounds and had experienced similar challenges.

After we were probably eight or nine months into the business, I was sitting with my uncle back in Atlanta, and he asked, "So what is your next goal?"

I thought about it and replied, "Well, my next goal is to get this hotel up and running more. I think we can get it to do $130,000 a month. And I think we can really get this hotel to the next level."

He shook his head and replied, "I'm very, very disappointed in you."

"Why?" I asked. "What do you mean?"

"You're not ambitious enough," he said.

Come on. I was living on this property, working every minute. I wasn't sleeping, and I wasn't ambitious enough? "What else should I be doing?" I asked.

"You should be thinking about going for the next hotel. What are you talking about getting this hotel up and running more? You need to focus on expanding your business."

I got the message.

"Okay," I said.

"Good," he told me. "Let's start looking for another property."

We called our accountant again, and my uncle said, "Do you have any other deals out there that we could look at in Atlanta? Could you check with your broker friend regarding any potential deals for us?"

The broker got back to us right away and said there was a hotel in Marietta, Georgia, called the Comfort Inn.

This was an operating business, and we purchased it on the spot, renaming it the Economy Hotel, Marietta. My uncle was still in town, and now, because we had added this second hotel, we started having to split up efforts. With our first purchase, I had been working at the front desk from six in the morning until ten at night. Then I put a note at the outside of the hotel every night to give customers who were coming in after ten o'clock my cell phone number so I could come out of my room and check them in. I didn't want to miss any potential customers between the hours of ten and six in the morning.

Once we acquired the new hotel, I still stayed on the front desk, but then I worked from six in the morning to four in the afternoon. After that, I jumped in my truck, headed to the other hotel, and got there by five. Then I worked at the front desk as well as managed the property until eleven o'clock each night. At the end of my shift, I would jump back into my truck, drive back to the first hotel, put the note outside, and did that whole thing over again. And I lived that routine for approximately a year and a half. My life was the hotels.

As you can see, my life had changed drastically from when I was earning a great salary, wearing a suit to work, and selling memberships to executives. I was living in Georgia, operating two hotels, and learning so much about business, about people, and about myself.

The first lesson I learned is personal. That is simply that I was never going to have bigger cheerleaders than my family. My family has and continues to be my ultimate support team. Second, I learned that you reap what you sow. You need to plant those seeds of working seven days a week, twenty hours a day before you can reap rewards. We often want to reap the rewards before we've done anything, and we talk ourselves into acting like and maybe even thinking that we've done something. Remember, you can't reap rewards without planting those seeds.

Lori Greiner, who has invented more than six hundred products and is a cast member of the Emmy-winning reality TV show *Shark*

Tank, says, "Entrepreneurs are willing to work eighty hours a week to avoid working forty hours a week."[4]

I would amend that to say *successful* entrepreneurs. You have to work and work hard.

Finally, you need to have supportive people around you. Not everyone has a family like mine, but anyone can create a circle of people who are going to be supporters of each other's dreams. Again, it goes back to the community. We all have friends or even family members who have so many insecurities that they are going to shoot down all your ideas, dreams, and ambitions. You need to make a conscious effort to be around people who are positive, people who are going to support your efforts, and you need to be conscious about that. You need to break away from individuals who are going to try to put you down.

When I was working on the front desk twenty hours a day, dealing with the responsibilities and challenges that came along with those duties, it was difficult, and it might have been impossible without my having a vision for where I wanted it to go.

You need that vision supported by people around you, and you need them supporting that vision and talking that vision out with you. Now, if everyone around you is like, "Okay, what are you doing? You're just wasting your time. You're wasting your youth on this, and it's not going to go in the direction you want it to." I mean, how demotivating is that? It's not giving you the energy to keep wanting to make the sacrifices you must to succeed. But if you have people there like my family members, you are going to hear them say things like, "Look, let's work our butts off, and one day, we might be sitting at ten hotels,

---

4   Libby Kane, "*Shark Tank* Investor: 'Entrepreneurs Are the Only People Who Will Work 80 Hours a Week to Avoid Working 40 Hours a Week,'" *Business Insider*, July 13, 2016, https://www.businessinsider.com/lori-greiner-shark-tank-entrepreneurs-2016-7.

and you never know what can happen." That's someone buying into your vision, and now you want to go to work. Now you're motivated to go through those struggles. Sure, you can go it alone, but that is a rough road. When you are already expending all that mental and physical energy on the daily chores of business, that positive infusion of support can make all the difference.

The other component of what I learned, the social component, was the struggles and the challenges of our customer base. That and the need for affordable housing in Atlanta. As I mentioned earlier, just being there on the front desk, on the front line, working with people who need this type of housing day in, day out, simply underlined the importance. Finally, I came to a realization once again that people need a sense of community to really thrive, and they need to find a little happiness in the affordable housing side as much or maybe even more than anywhere else.

Lessons Learned

- In this business, pricing is key.

- Understand your customer base.

- Make a conscious choice to be around people who are going to support your efforts.

- People need a sense of community to really thrive, and you need a support network and/or family to succeed.

- Growth and growing pains are often synonymous, but as you'll see in the next chapter, growth in the right direction can actually make your job easier.

CHAPTER 4

GROWTH

*If you really want to do something, you'll find a
way. If you don't, you'll find an excuse.*

—Jim Rohn

When I think about our second hotel, I always recall this story and
what it taught me. The hotel was empty when we bought it, so we had
to come up with a way to start generating customers. I remembered
what had worked with the first hotel—low-cost rooms—and I truly
believed the customers would come if we could just reach them. With
our first hotel, we generated considerable traffic by putting out signs
advertising rooms for $25. If it worked once, maybe it would work
again.

At this point, the Comfort Inn sign was still on the building.
We went to FedEx, and we printed out about a hundred yard signs
advertising rooms for $25 a night, just as we did in Roswell. So there
are my uncle and I—close to midnight—placing those signs. We put
them out in front of the hotel, we put them around the corner of the
hotel, on nearby streets—anywhere we could attract visual traffic that
was close to the hotel.

After that hurried adventure, we returned to the Roswell location and turned in for the night. The next morning, around eleven o'clock, we arrived at our new purchase—and to our surprise, customers were lined up down the street and around the corner!

The staff we had inherited from the previous owner was there, all of them as shocked as we were. Truly, these people were flabbergasted. They looked at us as if to ask, "What the heck did you guys just do?"

We were thrilled. This turnout just solidified our belief and our understanding that this affordable housing segment was really something Atlanta needed.

The Vision Grows

My job duties didn't improve; they only multiplied. I was just thinking to myself, *Well, I've come all the way over here, and I'm putting in all these hours, and my quality of life and my standard of living have gone down. So what have I actually gained? I left a beautiful city (Vancouver, Canada) where I had a six-figure salary that required me to travel across the country. I lived in a big home and enjoyed being close to friends and family. All of a sudden, I'm working twenty-hour days in a tough environment, living in a one-bedroom apartment, completely isolated. My only friend is the TV in the hotel lobby.* I'm sure most entrepreneurs feel that way at the beginning. When you've worked hard, pushed yourself beyond your own limits, and don't feel like you're thriving, you're going to have moments when you question yourself. Fortunately, I had developed a powerful self-talk that, to this day, gets me over the rough spots. I always remind myself that what I'm doing is temporary and that I am simply traveling through a time tunnel. More about that time tunnel later.

At this time, with ownership of the second hotel, my anxiety dissipated because my vision was a lot bigger. Now, instead of capping at one hotel and living behind that hotel's front desk for the rest of my life, I could see the larger opportunity. Now we were actually growing something as a business directive, and I was growing as well, both personally and professionally.

We purchased that second hotel from someone with multiple financial issues, one of which was an inability to pay the bank his monthly mortgage. He also was having his Comfort Inn franchise pulled away from him because he had not kept the hotel up to the company's standards.

So did we keep it as a Comfort Inn, or did we rename it? At first, I thought we should keep that highly recognizable name. I then talked it over with my uncle. His London bed-and-breakfasts were independent, and he strongly believed in the value of staying independent and running the business on our own terms versus being accountable to a third party. As time went on, I realized the wisdom of what he was saying.

That solidified, in my mind, the fact that I did not want to have anyone in charge of my destiny from a franchise perspective. I wouldn't want a third party coming in and telling me how to run the business or saying they were going to pull my flag. Those are a few reasons we stayed independent and have created our own franchise, the Economy Hotel brand.

At that time, between the two locations, we had about twenty-five employees.

The staff we inherited was good, but they were overwhelmed. Now they had one hundred customers to deal with. Within the next couple of weeks, we needed to find and hire all new staff because the ones we had just couldn't keep up with the demand coming through the door.

For the first few weeks, we were going by the other name, and then eventually we switched over to the Marietta Hotel.

This hotel was a little bit different in that it had full kitchens, which was an advantage. In the affordable housing segment, obviously a main component of affordability is being able to cook at home, so now that this had full kitchens, it worked with our customer base a lot better.

The Third Hotel

We ran that hotel for about a year, and then a broker approached us about a potential deal in Decatur, Georgia. This castle-like building had been empty for a couple of years. It had been used in the 1981 film *Cannonball Run*, starring Burt Reynolds and Farrah Fawcett.

We ended up getting it at a really great price. I approached family members and asked if they would be willing and able to invest in the project. Based on the track record of success with the first two hotels, they indicated that they were very interested in looking at getting involved in this third venture.

Summing up everything I knew about the location, it seemed like it would make sense to purchase, because the area where the hotel was located clearly needed affordable housing. The hotel was right off the highway, so it was very accessible. Then the purchase price of the asset was excellent. It was less than $800,000 for a one hundred–room hotel, which was an amazing price for something in metro Atlanta at the time.

If you buy that asset and you try to market to the Ritz-Carlton customer, it's just not going to work. But if you're buying it and you're marketing it to the right target customer base, you're going to get a lot more traction. That was our focus. By then, I knew our customer base, not just as demographics but as people. I knew what they needed, and I believed this hotel could deliver that.

Twenty Pages and a Lot of Time

This is probably the time to say that any investment should come with a lot of due diligence. It's also the time to say that, with this property, I didn't do all of my due diligence the way I should have. Roswell—both the county and the city—had been easy to deal with, and I didn't consider that some counties are a little bit harder and have more restrictions than others. I didn't realize all that it would take to get a business license, get an occupancy permit for the property, and get it up and running.

We went to the local county and basically said, "Hey, we'd like to get this hotel up and running. What are the steps that we have to take?"

They gave us about twenty pages of improvements that we needed to have done before we could get an occupancy permit. Those tasks ranged from getting architectural drawings to getting a green light from the local fire marshals to having code enforcement come in and sign off on the hotel as a safe place for people to stay. Delaying the opening and losing eight months of revenue caused us to nosedive into the red. We did not gauge all that when we initially bought the hotel, so this was a huge learning curve for me. Ultimately, a learning curve is a good thing. Since then, I've known what to expect and what questions to ask at the outset. I still would have purchased that hotel. I just would have been better prepared to estimate when we would be able to open it for business.

Creating a Team from Scratch

In the hospitality industry, managing investment properties is a challenge. According to the Bureau of Labor Statistics, in 2018, hotels and motels experienced a staff turnover rate of almost 74 percent. HR experts agree that a normal range should be as low as 10 to 15 percent.[5] Reasons for this turnover include a labor market with more job openings than employees and scheduling conflicts in what is basically a twenty-four-hour business. Yet, if you are going to be successful in this business, you have to understand your employees just as you understand your customer base.

Some decisions are made for you. They are created by circumstances, and you have no choice but to react. That was my situation—operating two hotels, and then this third hotel, which we needed to get running from the ground up. There are only twenty-four hours in a day, and I knew I couldn't be in charge of the front desk at both of our hotels as well as trying to get this old/new hotel of ours up and running. I was faced with the challenge of building a team, a strong one, so I could start delegating and getting more things accomplished. Once we acquired the third hotel, I took myself off the front desk, and I started hiring managers, placing them at the hotels, and building the human infrastructure we had already acquired. Doing that freed me up to oversee this new project.

> The major component of human resources is that word *human*—the human component.

In my previous jobs, I had been around a lot of great leaders, and I had read

---

5   Megan Wells, "Turnover and Retention Rates for Hotels and the Hospitality Industry," *Daily Pay* (blog), November 18, 2018, https://www.dailypay.com/blog/staff-turnover-rates-hotel-motel-hospitality-industry/.

a great deal about business, management, and building teams. I think the major component of human resources is that word *human*—the human component. When you're dealing with humans, you will have challenges. Finding resources challenges all of us who are building teams, because everyone is different. As a leader, you've got to be that person who is putting things together systematically and in a way that is both efficient and harmonious within the team.

Initially, my previous experience did help in terms of trying to build the team and find the right leaders. When I first started hiring, I had placed too much importance on past experience in the hotel industry, and I think that was a mistake.

For example, I hired a general manager who had worked previously at a major luxury hotel. I told myself, "Well, this person has worked at that hotel. She's going to be able to bring in a whole bunch of great new ideas and processes to help us change how we're doing things."

However, I didn't realize this person, despite her qualifications, was not going to be a fit because she did not understand our customer base. This was a different world for her. She had a difficult time adjusting and didn't last very long.

So I switched gears and started to look for management and employees who were coming from the multifamily world, specifically from property management of apartment complexes in some of the areas of Atlanta where tenants were similar in needs to our customer base.

Those employees could bring their instincts to the table, and that really helped us in developing our core infrastructure for future hires.

I don't mean any disrespect here. Quite the contrary. In the affordable housing segments, you're dealing with a specific and unique type of customer base, and the more you understand that base, the better you can serve them. Your customer base is typically already going through a lot of social and economic challenges. It takes experience and a special type of person to be able to deal with and help and work with those individuals. Each one comes with a different set of problems than, for example, a business traveler. I soon realized that someone with that past experience who could empathize and really be a resource for people going through these challenging times was what we wanted to start looking for and recruit. For example, we hired managers from a Doubletree that was across the street from one of our hotels. They knew our neighborhood and hotel, but after two years, they just stopped coming to work.

Our residents were born into an environment with a whole set of challenges. When that customer comes to work and hands over the money that he or she made at a minimum wage job that day in order to have a place to spend the night, they are not in the same emotional place as the business traveler or someone who is on vacation.

Today, I have more experience and more options in hiring. As I point out in a recent article for the *Atlanta Business Chronicle*, partnering with nonprofit organizations can be an excellent way to find employees. Shelters to Shutters, an Atlanta-based nonprofit, works with private employers to help qualified people find steady employment. Most important, it also works with homeless individuals, helping them reorient to the workforce while providing them with subsidized accommodation. A few years ago, an out-of-state couple visited one of my company's hotels seeking both work and a place to live. Although they could not afford rent, they possessed strong renovation skills and offered to help us maintain our properties in return for room and board. Within two years, the couple saved enough money to move themselves and their children into a bigger house, register their own construction company, and work as our preferred vendor on construction contracts. That was win-win for them and for us. Regardless of your business, you can seek out nonprofits that align with the same causes and serve the same purpose as your company. A successful, steady workforce helps spur the local economy and thus benefits the community in which it is based.

Networking with others in your field will also keep you aware of hiring practices and those who may be thinking of changing jobs. Now that our company has a team in place, we are better able to focus on the *human* in human resources and place the right person in the position that fits his or her skills. Although these personnel responsibilities will never be paint-by-number experiences, they are much easier than building a team from scratch as we did with that hotel.

For eight months, I worked on our new purchase. That's how long it took to get it up and running, dealing with contractors, trying to put together a team of employees, getting all the hotels in compliance, including making sure the rooms were clean and free of any sort of health hazards. Remember, the hotel had been down for a couple of years, and now we had to provide the county proof of compliance with everything related to the ordinances. Ultimately, we needed to start from scratch and get the whole property in a place it had not been even close to in years.

Although the first hotel had not been in great shape when we bought it, we were able to get it up and running in about four months. With the second hotel, they just handed over the keys to us, and we took over. It was beautiful.

The Importance of a Time Cushion

Not so with our third hotel. Not only was the start-up time double the time of the first one, but I had the additional challenge of investors, who, because of the success of the first two hotels, were scratching their heads and saying, "What's going on? We're used to money coming in pretty quickly, and here we are eight months later, and nothing has happened."

With that, I learned yet one more lesson. The situation opened my eyes to the fact that sometimes in our projections, we need to build in some cushion, and we need to be very realistic with our investors on what the potential timelines are going to be when getting an asset like this.

More Challenges

Finally, we had our license and operating permit. I even had a manager in place, and we were good to go. Still, more challenges arose. We didn't realize how tough the market was going to be in that area. We were dealing with a lot of elements in the local community that didn't work for us and would not work for our customer base. Once more, we had gone down the same path of offering rooms at $25 a night, and all of a sudden, we had a whole influx of customers coming in, which was awesome at first. Unfortunately, some of those customers were gang members or people involved in activities that would create problems for us and our other residents.

Different areas of any city have a completely diverse demographic. An area like Roswell, for instance, had a lot of individuals who were employed but whose salaries were not high enough to pay for an apartment in such a high-rent area. Those Roswell tenants tended to be more middle-aged, whereas the demographic in the new area was a little bit younger. They were twenty-one to twenty-five years old, and with that age range comes other issues. True, they needed affordable housing, but they were changing the environment of our hotel, and not for the better. We needed to get more older guests in the door, people who needed affordable housing and who were similar to the residents of our other hotels.

If I could go back in time, I would've probably started security from day one and made it a priority in terms of investment. But until we opened the third hotel and I got a grasp of the potential negative element that could be brought to the hotels, I didn't know we needed to bring in security full time.

I used to count the cash around noon every day. Anyone who was watching me could see what I was doing. And they could see when I was leaving with that cash and taking it to the bank. One day, I went through this counting ritual and decided there wasn't enough to take to the bank just then. So I picked up my laptop and headed toward the door. As I was walking out, I couldn't help but notice a guy in the lobby who was arguing and making a lot of noise. I tried to reason with him, and we went outside. Just then, almost as soon as we stepped through the door, I felt something cold against the back of my head. The guy who'd been arguing shouted and ran away, and I realized another guy behind me had a gun.

"Walk back in the lobby," he said as he swore in a steady stream.

Then he grabbed my laptop and ran away.

Call it luck, good fortune, or whatever, but just then, a police car was heading into the parking lot. The police officer saw the man running off and started following him. The guy dropped the laptop and his gun and took off.

The officer brought my laptop back to me. Then he said something I'll never forget.

"He had a gun," the officer told me.

"I know," I said.

"And the gun was loaded."

With one click, my life could have ended. One click. Coming from Canada, where legislation makes it more difficult for people to carry guns, I hadn't thought about this danger as seriously as I should have. That put everything in perspective for me. It really changed the way I looked at how we were operating.

As much of an eye-opener for me as this was, what further confirmed our need for security was my realization that what happened to me wasn't an isolated incident. We were getting more resident complaints about security, more loitering after hours. Rooms were being broken into at night.

Within the first week, we realized that we needed to both secure the building and change the customer base in a way that still provided affordable accommodation but to our true customer base. We put our heads together to figure out how we would do that, and the solution was twofold.

First of all, we started implementing twenty-four-hour security at the property. It was the first time we put security in place. Then we changed the pricing for this specific hotel, not significantly, only so we had our target customer base coming through the door—people who needed affordable accommodations but who were not doing anything illicit or illegal.

Microscaling the Model

After the third hotel, we had developed an effective framework of a business model to microscale the business. And I want to use that term. I wouldn't say just scale, because scaling can mean a lot of different things. McDonald's, for instance, is a macroscale, meaning they scale across the globe in a very massive fashion. When you've been around that long, you get to the position where you can do that.

We are still at a stage of microscaling, meaning we're continuously growing the company, but we're doing it very thoughtfully and very strategically. And we're still doing it one property at a time. After the fourth hotel, we microscaled to another three hotels. These were mom-and-pop operations, where the owners were ready to exit the company and they did not have a second generation who wanted the business. This is typical when you are dealing with older (what are known as C class) assets. The owners aren't going to have everyone in their family or their neighbors clamoring to take over their business when they retire. That's not because there's anything wrong with these assets. It's because most people don't see beyond the surface to the potential.

Recognizing the Potential

Ninety-nine percent of people just drive by these older (C or D class) properties and don't see what I see—first, a strong cash flow for the investor, and second, the number of jobs that property can produce, the changes and the income it can bring to the neighborhood and surrounding businesses, and, most of all, they don't see all the people who otherwise might be sleeping under a bridge without that accommodation.

Many times, the owners of these properties don't realize the potential of the asset that they're sitting on. For instance, the owners of most of the hotels we acquire, the mom-and-pops, have closed down half or more of the rooms in the hotel. They do this because it's hard for only two or three people to manage a one hundred–room property, so they just close down rooms because it's easier for them to manage fifty than to figure out what to do with one hundred. But that's where their cash flow is, and the challenge with their approach is that it is cutting out half their inventory.

The product they're selling is hotel rooms, and when they cut out half of that inventory, they are going to lose money. That has been the situation with almost every acquisition we've seen.

Volume versus Room Rates

Once we buy a property, the first thing I do is look at how many of the rooms need to be opened, and we just go and do that. Within thirty days, we open up all the rooms. Once you have more product, that enables you to shift your price point, because now you're selling in volume, which has been the goal from the start. When you go from selling fifty rooms to one hundred rooms, you can instantly bring down your daily rates by half, just as we did in the first hotel at $25 a night. Then you can focus on selling your rooms in terms of volume versus room rates.

When you can focus on selling your rooms in volume, your occupancy will go up very quickly, because the need for affordable accommodation is going to be there in any market you go to.

That's basically what happens step by step. We acquire the asset, we turn it into affordable accommodation, we open up the rooms, we fill those rooms, and within six months, we should be in the black, and we just go forward from there.

Lessons Learned

- Build in that time cushion, and know that sometimes it might take a little while to get a property up and running. Let your investors know, especially if your previous investments didn't take that long to provide a return. Simply put, manage expectations of investors and of anyone involved in the profit and loss of the business.

- Understand the importance of building an HR infrastructure, and learn how to delegate—that was definitely very important for me.

- Third and equally important is that you ensure that you do your due diligence in any of the markets you enter—and fully understand the pros and cons of entering that market. This due diligence goes beyond profit and loss to consider all the other implications. What's the local economy like? What's the local market like? What's the local demographic like? Who's going to stay at our hotels, and what is our plan to house those individuals if they do stay at our hotels?

- Investigate the value of outsourcing, which is what we did with the security at our hotels.

- Work at microscaling your business, one investment at a time.

- View potential investments—beyond the surface—to what is possible.

That experience taught me many lessons about my chosen career and about myself. In addition to learning ground-up lessons of investing, I've also learned personal lessons that are just as important. I hope they help you as you embark on your own journey. As you'll see in the next chapter, much of what happens to us is out of our control, and we must decide how we are going to react to adversity, not *after* but *before* it happens.

CHAPTER 5

PERSONAL LESSONS

About two years before I started writing this book, the local news station in Atlanta came out to one of our hotels. I was in London at the time, but that didn't stop them. I was getting calls from my employees saying the news anchor and camera crew had come by the hotel. They were trying to catch me getting out of my car so they could run up to interview me.

Finally, I got an email from the reporter. I emailed them back, saying, "I'm out of town. I'm happy if people want to come down, and I can talk to you when I return."

Instead, by the time I came back, the station had already run the segment, a piece on all types of extended-stay hotels in Atlanta, saying that these business owners were housing criminals and they were also housing children in the same buildings. The angle was that the business owners cared only about making money and that they were disregarding the people to whom they rented. Worse, without speaking to me, without learning anything about our business, they made assumptions about me that were far from the truth.

A Punch in the Gut

I came back to town, and here I was all over the news along with a distorted image of what our hotels are really all about. The story was made up of half truths and a lack of thorough reporting, angled and manipulated in a way that made business owners, me included, look bad. I'm not sure why they did it that way, but they didn't go after the facts. They set up the story to get the most sensational end product.

That was really a punch in the gut for me, especially because I was known for trying to help the people who lived in our hotels. Yes, we were going to have incidents that I couldn't control. That was unavoidable in the affordable housing segment. But I cared greatly about the well-being of our residents, and now my name was out there in a negative light, and my reputation was on the line. I couldn't do anything because someone else was controlling the narrative.

They could have—and should have—dug much deeper into what's really going on with hotels like mine. Had they looked at the overall picture, they would have understood that in the affordable housing segment, if you're housing three thousand people a night, especially people who are going through socioeconomic challenges, the reality is, there's probably going to be an issue with a few of them. Instead of focusing on that alone, they could have looked at the overall picture and asked themselves, "What service is that business providing for the local community?"

Well, first of all, it is providing affordable accommodation. It is providing a service that enables shelters to avoid overcrowding, because if they were not staying with us, many of these people might not even have a bed to sleep on. They don't have the credit or the money for a deposit to rent in an apartment complex. So where else could they go?

That very day I returned, I went into action. It's just a natural reaction for me if I feel I've been punched to want to punch back. I was not going to take that blow without reacting and certainly not just going to accept that they're saying things about me that weren't true.

The first thing we did was go online and respond to a lot of the comments that were being made about my being a slumlord. Others on my staff pushed back as well. Then I contacted a public relations company. My attitude regarding the media was, "No, we are not going to let you guys dictate what our image is going to be. We'll put our own image out there, and we'll let the public decide."

I knew we had to be proactive in vocalizing what we stand for because if we didn't, then everyone else was going to be able to make up their own scenarios.

I'm telling you this story because, for me, it was a personal nightmare, and in the course of your career, you will have nightmares of your own. I'm actually glad it happened because it taught me that I need to control the narrative of what our company is about and what we stand for. That's exactly what we started doing after that. Our public relations firm began getting articles in major publications, including our local newspapers. We increased our social media presence. We published blogs about our residents and our employees. Here's the crazy part. I would not have done any of this if it hadn't been for that feature piece on my business. I have the media to thank for the fact that I got actively involved in spreading the word about what we do and what we stand for.

That's a major lesson I've learned and one I hope you take from this book. Sometimes when you get punched in the

> Sometimes when you get punched in the gut, you can turn that into an opportunity to progress.

gut, you can turn that into an opportunity to progress. You need to be proactive and then ask yourself what you can do and how you can collectively convert the negative situation into a value for yourself and your company.

The Tool of Self-Assessment

I did more than just get my true story out there. I also did some reflecting. Self-assessment is a great tool. Some of the ways you can and should assess yourself include the following:

- Your productivity skills

- Your people skills

- Your communication skills

- Your finance skills

- Your work-life balancing skills

After a crisis, you especially need to do some serious reflecting. That's what I did. How could I have avoided this? What could I have done better? I always think that although we can't be social workers, maybe there is something that we can do to help the people living in our hotels. Maybe there's something extra we can create on site that will help them through. It could be something as simple as putting out pamphlets on mental health and public services on the front desk.

If you take a lesson out of each of those problems you've experienced, and if you attach an action to it—such as the pamphlets, which I actually did put out—then you can realize something positive has come out of that situation.

A Tunnel of Time

If I could give you any final advice on the personal side of what I've learned, it would be this: take a long-term view. Just as in the real estate market, you are going to experience a lot of ups and downs in your personal life. Try to take the long-term view and understand that no one investment or no one specific circumstance is going to dictate where you can be in three to five years. Many times, we tend to forget this in our day-to-day activities, and it's extremely important. When I first came to Atlanta, living in the hotel, basically working twenty-four hours a day, every day, if I hadn't taken that long-term view, I could have easily let depression set in. But I knew there was light at the end of the proverbial tunnel. That's how I think of it—a time tunnel. You just have to get through it.

When I reflect on my day-to-day operational life over the last eight years, I look back at any number of situations that challenged me. If you don't have a vision of where you want to be, you'll find it difficult to pull through. You have to be able to tell yourself that this is just a tunnel of time that you have to walk through to be better than you were before. That's what I do. As actor Gregory Peck said, "Tough times don't last; tough people do."

The Value of Self-Talk

Talking to yourself is a good thing. Really. Self-talk works for me, and I speak to myself the way I would to a good friend. "Look," I say. "You're walking through a tunnel right now. It's going to be a month or two months of you getting your ass kicked, and you're going to have to deal with it."

We are constantly pushed in life. If you think that what is happening to you now is going to be the constant, you're dooming yourself from the start. One of the most difficult things to do is talk yourself out of that feeling that where you are is permanent. It's just part of a cycle. Yet, as long as you recognize there's a tunnel there, you can do it.

Remember, self-talk is influenced by your subconscious mind, and you're going to have it regardless. When you're going through a crisis, that self-talk could be negative if you don't step in and take charge of it. You could be unnecessarily blaming and beating up on yourself. You could be thinking this is the end of the world, when really it's just a major bump in your path.

Self-talk can enhance your performance and general well-being. For example, research shows self-talk can help athletes with performance. It may help them with endurance or to power through a set of heavy weights. Furthermore, positive self-talk and a more optimistic outlook can have other health benefits, including the following:

- Increased vitality

- Greater life satisfaction

- Improved immune function

- Reduced pain

- Better cardiovascular health

- Reduced risk for early death

- Less stress[6]

Sometimes, for me, self-talk is as simple as saying, "Hey, this is easy. Take a deep breath. There's something you can learn out of this to make your business and yourself better."

---

6   Kimberly Holland, "Positive Self-Talk: How Talking to Yourself Is a Good Thing," Healthline.com, updated June 26, 2020, https://www.healthline.com/health/positive-self-talk.

I remind myself of where I am, that it's temporary, and I push myself through that tunnel, knowing it's going to be better on the other end. And it always is.

It will be better for you as well.

Challenges, Bigger Rewards

Nothing forces you to truly know yourself and others the way becoming a from-the-ground-up entrepreneur does. You are tested daily, sometimes hourly. You are playing for high stakes in a game that offers big rewards and involves taking big chances. You live knowing your decisions can make or break you and affect the lives of others. You put in ridiculously crazy hours, and you push yourself beyond where you think your limits are. Then you get up the next day and do it again. In the moments between all that frenetic activity, you look at something you created from scratch—from the ground up. You think about the people you have helped and the way you have grown, and, in that moment, you're grateful and at peace. I can't think of a more exciting, more fulfilling way to live.

Lessons Learned

- If you start moving forward and start pushing yourself—now—the blessings will find you.

- Practice self-assessment, especially after a crisis.

- Regardless of where you are located, remember every real estate market has unique advantages to it.

- If you get punched in the gut—and you will—try to find the lesson in it and a way to turn it around.

- If you don't take charge of your self-talk, it will take charge of you.

- Know that when you're going through a challenge, you are in a tunnel of time, and you won't be there forever.

So, yes, you will deal with challenges, and certainly those lessons will be as much, probably more, about you as they are about business. But now that you know more about what lies ahead and how to deal with it, let's dig a little deeper. Part of personal development is growing into a strong leader, so that you can create and build a strong team. That's what we're going to look at next.

CHAPTER 6

BUILDING THE TEAM

*Get the right people on the bus, the wrong people off
the bus, and the right people in the right seats.*

—James C. Collins

This may sound ironic, but the larger our company became, the easier it was to manage. During this time, we were growing the management team and learning how to work with a larger team from across the city as opposed to the way we had been operating one or two hotels. Now we had staff placed in multiple cities throughout Georgia. Right away, I could see that we needed to figure out the best way to be on top of various issues and be able to communicate at all times as we grew.

One of the strategies we started using was group chats through WhatsApp. We put all our managers and all our employees in these group chats. We were able to communicate consistently through them, and everyone could know what everyone else was doing and could hold each other accountable for things happening at each of the locations.

Regardless of whatever else was going on in the company, these chats have created a sense of community because early every day, everyone gets up and jumps in a group chat and says good morning to each other.

Then someone might say, "There's a problem going on at my hotel. I need help with this."

A manager from one property might ask for advice—or offer it—to the manager of another property.

Without my realizing it at first, this instant communication started developing twenty-four-hour group chats across our various hotels. Connecting everyone created a community within the company, and I started to see how the power of having the right people in the right seats alongside having everyone row in the same direction through these communication channels could work for us.

It may sound very simple or even weird to people who haven't tried it, but this practice is more than just starting group chats. It's about sharing, about being connected. Instant messaging was the way I communicated with the people in my life, and it made sense to extend that to my company. I'm glad I did.

Leadership speaker Mark Sanborn puts it this way: "In teamwork, silence isn't golden; it's deadly." We didn't have silence and didn't have all the challenges that go with it. Regardless of what was going on, everyone was on board and trying to participate and solve problems from the moment they went to work until they finished for the day.

Around this time, I was getting a little bit more of a work-life balance. My duties had transitioned by necessity, and I had moved out of that first hotel and was managing all of them. We had leveraged out a lot of our six managers to other properties, and with that delegating as well as outsourcing, I was spending less time going between the assets myself, trusting the team to handle many of the duties I had performed when I was the only one who could.

At this point, we were running our day-to-day operations and keeping the business plan pretty much the same. Then we went for the fourth property, Economy Hotel Airport.

I had found this hotel on LoopNet, a website where hotels are listed for sale. After finding this property, I called the real estate agent and asked him to give me a viewing. I saw the property, I went to look at it, and I thought it was going for a really good price. It was right by the airport, so the price point as well as the location seemed ideal. The next step was putting in the offer. And that was it. We purchased it, and we were excited about the opportunity that it might add to our portfolio. It was important from a land value perspective because property that is close to an airport is attractive for other potential investors, and that would matter if we ever decided to sell it in the future.

Growing Pains? Growing Gains

Now we had enough management personnel and others in infrastructure to really manage the properties. As I said above—and it surprised me at first—the more our company grew, the easier it was to manage. With more resources and more revenue coming into the company, we could reinvest into our managers and our people infrastructure.

When you can delegate the right way, you'll find it actually becomes easier to run a business that has grown, for three important reasons. First, you have more cash flow coming in. Second, you have more people to help, and third, you have more eyes that are on top of what they're doing. If you can create accountability at various levels, that's a major step.

Organic Accountability

Direct reports are essential, and you need to make sure you're managing them. For instance, I manage about six or seven direct reports at all times. Below them, each of my direct reports has three or four direct reports of their own. And those people have one or two direct reports. Everyone on a micro and macro level has to manage the people underneath them. There's tremendous power in accountability, and I've found direct reports are the easiest, most respectful, and most organic way to establish that accountability.

I also implemented something in our organization called the Entrepreneurial Operating System, an idea I got from Gino Wickman's book *Traction: Get a Grip on Your Business,* which I'll discuss in more detail shortly. The book breaks down the management and infrastructure within an organization from the standpoint of accountability.

It shows how to create a vision for your company, how to create core values and core processes, and how to have a core focus. It also helps you organize different aspects of your business with, for example, an accountability chart. This chart, which is similar to an organizational chart, provides you with the opportunity to place people on paper where they can best leverage their strengths. Everyone in the company knows what they're accountable for. Then, as the organization grows, it's a lot easier to manage because you have people who know, within their silos, what they're supposed to be doing every day.

Having said that, I don't think managing people is a perfect science for any entrepreneur. You can have the most detailed accountability chart, but you still have to hold everyone accountable for what they're doing. The human dynamic usually comes down to the simple fact that you are going to get performers, and you're going to get nonperformers, and you don't know if you're going to have a nonperformer until at least ninety days into someone's employment. Once you start seeing who is a performer and who's not, as a leader, you really have to be able to take action and make sure you have the right person in the right seat.

When I say right seat, I mean that you've created a position that the company truly needs. For example, we needed a finance and administration manager because we needed someone to manage those functions. That's the right seat, a seat that needs to be filled.

The Right Fit

What happens when you have the right seat but the wrong person? I think the best thing that you can do for people who are not going to work out for your company is fire them as soon as you can, because if you don't fire them, you're not doing them any service. What you're doing is basically holding them back from something that they could be potentially great at in another role or another organization.

The second component is, How do you fill that seat with the right person? You've got to analyze what type of person and what skill sets you need for that seat to be filled with the right individual, and you make a list of all the qualities you're looking for. In the case of the finance and administrative hire, it might be that they're organized; it might be that they're good with numbers and paperwork. Then, when you're interviewing the people for this position, they have to hit all those check marks. If they do, then you've gotten past the first step of hopefully finding the right person for the right seat. Every ninety days after that, you sit down with them and discuss where they are in terms of performance.

Are they doing everything they need to be doing to make that position successful, or are they slipping somewhere? If you address it regularly enough, I think you can nip problems in the bud before they fester too long and grow into bigger problems. That's why it's really important. With each of the positions we have, I perform these checks, and I ask my managers to do the same with their direct reports, both weekly and quarterly.

The weekly meetings point out potential strengths and issues right away, and then the quarterly meeting is an overview of what your progress is—just how you are doing. We really believe in giving our managers consistent feedback so they know on the map of responsibilities how they're achieving overall.

In one situation, the person we hired was from a large real estate investment trust. Her role was to come into the organization to manage a lot of the financial components of the company. On paper, as many people often are, she was awesome. She had all the skill sets you could imagine. She knew how to put together funds, how to manage paperwork, and how to manage budgets. In short, I believed her great tangible skill sets on paper would translate really well into that role. And so, we had the right seat, which was the position; we needed to get the right person; and we thought she would be the one.

Over the next thirty days, we began to see problems, and we realized that she came from a corporate culture that was very large. Many times in large corporations, you'll have people who go on an extended lunch break, come in a little bit later or leave a little bit earlier, and have long conversations over their coffees, and although this wastes a lot of time, no one really notices. However, we're a small company in many ways, and in our environment, if someone is not pulling their weight, they're going to be called out right away.

After this person left, we promoted someone from within who was below that rank. We moved her up into that position, and she did a great job.

The Lists

Over a thirty-day period, we have something called a weekly to-do list for all our managers. Every week, our managers leave with a to-do list of five or six things that they have to get done by the next meeting. If they don't complete the items on their list by the next weekly meeting, they have to report to the entire team, not just to me, on why they did not get their items done or which item did not get done and what happened. By the fourth week, when the employee I mentioned above had not done what she was supposed to be doing, she just left on her own.

Our environment doesn't allow that hiding of inefficiency or keeping that deadweight because employees' to-do lists point out who is working. If you complete the tasks on that list, no one's going to bother you. If you don't, you're going to be called out. In most cases, you won't even have to be called out because, at a certain point, you're going to say, "Look, this is not for me." You're not going to want to be embarrassed, and you'll want to find a company that is a better fit for what you want out of a job.

This structure really holds everyone accountable. The genius with the system is that you don't have to hold people personally accountable. You don't have to get into an argument with someone about why they're not doing their job. It's a team accountability situation, where you're coming to the team and telling them why you're not doing it. And there is leeway. Of course, situations out of control happen to all of us, and there will be times when someone can't complete all their items. But by the fourth week or the third week, if you have something that should've been done in a week that is not done, you better believe the team members are going to be scratching their heads and wondering why you're still working there. This accountability creates an environment where everyone is positioned to achieve, and if they don't achieve, they're going to be cycled out of the company on their own. They won't want to be there anymore because it's not a nice place to come to work if you're not accomplishing agreed-upon goals or pulling your weight.

Just as some people run from that kind of accountability, others thrive in those types of environments, and those are the ones we want joining our team. We want the person who's going to come to work and accomplish and feed the bigger picture of the vision for the company and take action on it as necessary.

Assessments

Although I've gotten better at hiring, I think people in general have become very skilled at the art of being interviewed. If you have the right things in your résumé, and if you can say the right things, you're probably going to get your foot in the door many times. We do use assessments now, and that's helped us do a better job at finding the right people for us. Each new manager candidate takes a strength-finders assessment, and that gives us insight into the strengths of that manager. If the strengths are focused around achievement and being proactive and they are doers, then that is something we want in the culture of the organization.

The questions are open ended, and there is no right or wrong answer. The candidate is asked how he or she would react in various situations, and all the choices are good ones. However, in some environments, those choices are going to be really useful, and in other environments, they will be less so.

If their strength finder comes back saying that they are creative, for example, and they're more of a learner, there's nothing wrong with that, but that's not great for our business; it's not really what we need.

We need someone who can roll up their sleeves from a management perspective, handle all types of situations, and get things done. The strength-finder assessment is an extra component we use after the interview to give us more insight into the candidate, so we can make sure, once again, we have the right person in the right seat.

Building toward Success

I had a strong belief that we would be super successful when we had our first hotel. And as we acquired more properties, and as we grew the business, my belief was solidified. Also, as we grew the business, my skill sets as a CEO increased and expanded. With that expansion, I was able to guide the direction of the company in a more cohesive manner. When we first started, I would have no idea about how to implement any of the systems we use now. Around the time we bought the fourth hotel, going into the next component of our business, growing it, and learning more about how to manage staff really helped us solidify how we were holding people accountable.

> You have to be able to let go of a lot of things, and you've got to be able to trust the people you've put in place to handle certain tasks.

When I transitioned from being a worker *in* the business to being a worker *on* the business, there was a shift. Not long before, I was running the day-to-day operations myself, and I had to learn how to develop a team so they could run it for me. In order to get to that point, you have to be able to let go of a lot of things, and you've got to be able to trust the people you've put in place to handle certain tasks. That's the only way that you can really scale a business.

As I write this book, we are negotiating the purchase of a new hotel out of state. Now, more than ever, I need a strong team. Three years ago I could not have even thought about expanding past Georgia. But now I'm very keen on doing that because we have the operational structures and people in place to help us get there.

Growing Talent, Giving It Time

Time is a crucial element here because the longer people are with you, and the longer you can develop that team, the likelihood of their being efficient enough to do the job is going to be a lot higher. Over time, they will experience enough scenarios that they'll be able to identify and fix problems when new ones arise. They'll be able to deal with new projects based on how they dealt with old ones.

As you're developing that team, you need to give them time to grow. As leaders, sometimes we underestimate the amount of time it takes for team members to grow into their positions. Most people take a lot of time. They are going to make mistakes, and you need to develop a patience level in order to see their skills come to fruition.

I have an operations manager and a revenue manager who, as of this writing, have been with the company for close to six years. Any time I purchase a hotel, they are qualified and experienced enough to go and open up that hotel for us. From top to bottom, they can and do implement all the core processes that we need to have in that hotel and get it functioning, probably within a couple of weeks. However, they developed those skills over the past six years. They didn't have that level of competency when they first joined our company, and I didn't expect them to. They learned from trial and error, by making and learning from mistakes, by day-to-day interaction with and feedback from me. You don't learn efficient hotel operation overnight.

One of our general managers started off as a security guard, and over time, looking at her develop and realizing what a responsible person she was, we gave her more responsibility. We put her on the front desk, and then we made her an assistant general manager. After that, we made her a general manager, and now she's general manager of two hotels.

We have another manager who began in housekeeping, and I'm really proud of that. It's remarkable to see how some people can grow into the opportunities that are put in front of them. We look for three characteristics, and those are the three core values of our organization: work ethic, a drive for continuous improvement, and integrity. It's pretty hard to hide those characteristics when you have them. People are going to notice someone with an excellent work ethic, someone who wants to come to work and be better than they were yesterday, and someone with integrity, someone we can trust to manage various aspects of the business when no one is looking.

From Hotel Resident to Front Desk Manager

As I mentioned earlier, working those early days at the front desk gave me an opportunity to get to know our residents, not just as demographics but as people. I got to learn a little of their stories as they learned a little of mine. Barbara was one of those people.

Her husband had just died from cancer. Because she didn't have the means to pay rent on their apartment, she and her daughter had moved into the hotel. She had a storm of dire straits happening in her life, and she started drinking. We talked, I learned more about her, and finally, I offered her the opportunity to take a job with the company.

Barbara started as a housekeeper, and she moved all the way up to a front desk manager. Her whole life took a turn for the positive.

Furthermore, her daughter just got into college. Think of the generational effect Barbara's success has had. Hers is an inspirational story, one the *Atlanta Journal Constitution* recently featured in an article.

Every once in a while, you meet someone like Barbara, who takes that opportunity and runs with it. And if we can have one of those like her for every hundred opportunities we offer, I'll be thrilled. Hers is probably one story of many in terms of people we've hired who lived at the hotel. Approximately 10 percent of the employees in our company have, at one time, been residents at one of our hotels.

Three Components

Getting the right person in the right seat really comes down to three components. Ask yourself the following:

1. Do they understand the job?

Does this person you hired really understand the job and how to do it? Can the person do the job without your having to actively do it for them or manage them? This is a component many employers—and employees—overlook at the beginning. Obviously, you can train someone on a job, but they have to have the intellectual capacity to understand what you're teaching them to do, and sometimes they may shine in other areas but lack the abilities to perform this specific job. On the other hand, sometimes an employee will surprise you and absolutely grasp what you're trying to teach.

2. Do they want the job?

Well, of course they do, they're going to tell you. But do they? This second component is major because, although a lot of people will take a job for a paycheck, that doesn't mean they're going to be happy in that job or even in that company.

3. Do they have the capacity?

Do they possess the capacity to do the job? Much of this component has to do with the logistics of their being able to do the job. For example, capacity for a job that entails an employee's driving around the city might mean asking, "Do you have a car? If you don't have a car, then you don't have the capacity to do that job."

These are the components I look for in the first ninety days of someone's employment. They are the questions you need to ask yourself, and you need to answer all three with *yes* to put the right person in the right place. Do they understand the job? Do they understand the components of the job? Can they do it well? Second, do they want the job? Do they have the motivation? Do they want to come to work every day, and are they going to be a positive influence on the corporate culture? Finally, are they going to have the capacity? Do they have the tools to get that job done?

In my business, if some otherwise qualified candidate says, "Well, I need to be home every night by five thirty because I need to have dinner with my family, and family life is really important to me," that's fantastic, and I completely respect that. However, we're a twenty-four-hour business.

When you work for us in certain positions, you can be sure that duties and situations are going to come up on your schedule at six or seven o'clock at night. As the leader and manager of that property, you're going to have to be there to perform those duties and handle those situations regardless of what time you're supposed to be somewhere else.

Our jobs cover the gamut. We're hiring everything from house-keepers to managers, positions with very different demands. Still, I think basing our hiring decisions on these three components has helped our retention across the board.

You also need a certain amount of flexibility—and humanity. When I first hired residents of our hotel, I looked for our core values in those people and tried to be as flexible as possible within the boundaries of the job. Bill Gates was right when he said, "The competition to hire the best will increase in the years ahead. Companies that give extra flexibility to their employees will have the edge in this area."

Networking Opportunities

I knew I had to do more than just manage hotels. I had to become a better manager. I had to network. And I needed to know others with challenges and successes similar to my own. At the end of the day, you can come home with your problems as a CEO, and you can talk to your spouse about them or you can talk to your friends or your family, but I think most leaders don't want to burden their families with their day-to-day problems at work. Even though your family members love you and want to be there for support, you, on the other hand, want to be the person providing for them. You want to be the strength behind the family.

The same is true with your employees. You don't want to be giving all your problems to the world. Furthermore, most family members won't truly understand your problems the way a peer group will.

Peer groups provide you with the opportunity to connect with people who are probably going through the same issues you are, and you can start developing solutions based on other people's past experiences. My personal growth benefited immensely when I joined two CEO peer mentoring groups, Vistage and Young President's Organization (YPO). CEOs meet monthly to share their concerns, their problems, and what's going right (and not so right) in their businesses and their personal lives.

These groups have helped me evolve as a leader. YPO and Vistage enabled me to learn from other people around the table and what they did in similar situations.

I'm sometimes asked how I found the time to join groups. I didn't find the time; I made the time. I just made a commitment to bettering myself as a CEO, and I saw this as the best way to do that—not only from a knowledge perspective and a way for me to communicate and learn from other CEOs, but over and above that, from a networking perspective, because I wanted to grow my business and use external funding one day. What better place to do that and build those relationships than in these kinds of CEO groups? These people have large networks, a high net worth, and high integrity. They are people I can and will do business with at some point, so the groups are also a networking opportunity for me.

The Best Teachers: Experience and Reading

Management is a constant state of growth and improvement, and I am passionate about learning. I had two powerful early mentors: my uncle, to whom I spoke just about every day on every step of my development, and my mom. It's amazing to see where they started, as immigrants, and what they achieved with their businesses, all without the investment funding I had. I respect them very much and value every conversation I have with them. Both have a wealth of knowledge, wisdom, and grit. Pete, the hotel owner who befriended me in so many ways when I was starting, was also instrumental, someone I called every couple of days. I tell you this to point out that you don't have to have more than a few important mentors. Before I joined the peer networking groups, when I needed input and opinions, I went only to family and Pete. I'll always be grateful for their advice.

Experience is definitely the best teacher, and it's a practical teacher, but there needs to be a theory behind it. Theory is good for the higher level of thinking and creativity you learn in books and in school. But then, the balance of that is practicality.

Sometimes I speak to young entrepreneurs who tell me about all the great ideas they have for launching new start-ups or new apps. But they often don't talk about, and sometimes don't seem to understand, the practical issues of how to really put all those ideas swimming around their heads into action. Sometimes our heads can get stuck in the clouds, thinking about how great our lives will be when we achieve success. Still, regardless of how great your ideas are, and especially regardless of how much money people are willing to invest in you, there must be a point when you just roll up your sleeves and do the work. Before you spend too much time with your head in the clouds, you need to keep your feet on the ground and start out by actually operating the business. That will teach you volumes. You'll also learn a great deal by reading, and I'm not just talking about the internet headlines.

Thirty Pages a Day: A Reading Goal

Speaking of volumes, in addition to mentors and hands-on experience, you need to read. That's the way I am able to process a great deal of knowledge, even on my busiest days. Reading is power. As I mentioned earlier, I wasn't the best student until I got serious about my work and my life. Now I love to read. At the end of the day, why make your own mistakes and try to learn from them when you can read a book and learn from someone else's mistakes and then navigate accordingly?

Reading can also inspire you, and sometimes the right inspiring story or example will be just what you need to motivate yourself to keep trying or look at a challenge in a different way. Consider the following:

- Bill Gates reads one book per week.

- Mark Zuckerberg reads one book every two weeks.

- Elon Musk is an avid reader. (At age nine, he's said to have read through the entire Encyclopedia Britannica. When asked how he knew so much about rockets, Musk told an interviewer, "I read a lot of books.")

- Warren Buffett spends about 80 percent of his day reading.

- Mark Cuban reads for more than three hours every day.[7]

This means you need to prioritize reading as an important part of your development. Mark Cuban, for instance, is a vocal supporter of treating business like a sport, which means he looks for the competitive edge however he can.

Cuban said daily reading worked wonders at the start of his career.

"Everything I read was public," he wrote in his blog's Success and Motivation Series. "Anyone could buy the same books and magazines. The same information was available to anyone who wanted it. Turns out most people didn't want it."[8]

If it works for people like Gates, Zuckerberg, and Cuban, it will work for you. I recently set a goal of reading thirty pages of a book a day. Typically, that gives me about two books a week. Once I started

---

7   "Why Entrepreneurs and Business Owners Should Read Books Regularly to be Successful," Theentrepreneurway.com blog, accessed August 3, 2020, http://theentrepreneurway.com/blog/why-entrepreneurs-and-business-owners-should-read-books-regularly-to-be-successful/.

8   Chris Weller, "9 of the Most Successful People Share Their Reading Habits," *Business Insider*, July 20, 2017, https://www.businessinsider.com/what-successful-people-read-2017-7.

this practice, I was amazed by how much I could learn in a year. Just set the goal—thirty pages a day—and imagine how many books you will have read at the end of this year. Compare this to the reading habits of the general population.

According to a 2018 study by Pew Research Center, about a quarter of American adults say they haven't read a book in whole or in part in the past year, whether in print, electronic, or audio form.

What could be an easier way to put your knowledge-gaining skills ahead of the game? Thirty pages a day. Two books a week. Just create that one new habit. Obviously, you are still going to make wrong decisions, even if you read one hundred books a week, but reading will help you potentially navigate away from some of the bigger mistakes you might have otherwise made.

If anyone had told me—even when I was in college—that I would be reading two books a week and looking forward to it, I hate to admit I would have laughed. When you start seeing the value of reading (and that comes only with actually doing it and then putting your knowledge to practical use), then you kind of become addicted to it.

Gino Wickman, successful business consultant, developer of the Entrepreneurial Operating System, and best-selling author of *Traction: Get a Grip on Your Business*, is one author whose books I have pretty much memorized. That's how helpful they are.

Changing Roles

As I mentioned before, you can read, you can plan, and you can think you're ready. Ultimately, however, if your business grows, as mine did, you have to turn over the day-to-day to people you trust to manage it. Trust is a tricky thing. In a large corporation, you as the hiring manager might believe in someone, but if they make a mistake—and some will—you can still go to the board of directors and point a finger at that person. You can still say, "Look, I just made a bad decision about whom I delegated to this position. Let's move on."

When you're the CEO and part owner of a company like mine, you have an extra challenge because the failure is more personal. Not only did you delegate the job to someone who did not accomplish what you asked them to do, but you're also taking a financial hit. So are those who believed enough in you to invest in your company. That connection makes you a lot more cautious about when you're delegating, and that financial issue is one component of it.

> When you grow a business from the ground up, and when you see it sprout into a flower, you have a certain affinity for that organization or that business, and it's almost like your child in many ways.

The other component is emotional. There's no way around that. When you grow a business from the ground up, and when you see it sprout into a flower, you have a certain affinity for that organization or that business, and it's almost like your child in many ways.

In his book, *Beyond Reservations: How a Family Root Beer Stand Grew into a Global Company*, J. W. Marriott Jr. tells how his father, the founder of the iconic hotel chain, wrote him a letter that details the how-to aspects of building a business. In his seventies, he is very much a hands-on CEO—so much so that 80 percent of his schedule involves visiting hotels around the country. He meets with his general managers and walks the hotels with them. Even though he's no doubt worth a few billion dollars, his concern is always that "baby" of his. He wants it to continue being successful.

That kind of hands-on attention is debatable, of course. If you pursue that type of management, you might want to succeed so badly that you become a helicopter parent to your business. When that happens to the extreme, you cannot delegate because you won't let the people to whom you're trying to delegate breathe. Yes, I've been guilty of that micromanagement. I think any from-the-ground-up CEO is. From time to time, I may still be guilty of it because so much is riding on proper management, not just for you but for everyone who trusts and depends on you. Maybe this business is a machine that's putting food on the table for one hundred or more people. You absolutely want to make certain you quarantine and correct any major mistakes immediately.

You can look at it two ways. One approach is Marriott's. As a founder, you just have that possessive, responsible feeling in you. The other way to look at it is what I'm striving for, and that is to encourage and not stifle innovation. You can't grow if the people who work for you are afraid to make mistakes.

I believe it's possible to both strive for innovation and make sure that you also have a pulse on your business. One of the biggest mistakes I've seen some of my peers make is delegating so much that they are really now distant from the business, and they don't know what's happening on the ground. Believe me, when something does happen on the ground, especially something catastrophic, you as the CEO still have to deal with the consequences, regardless of whether it was your mistake or the mistake of someone to whom you delegated responsibility. In the end, all problems are the CEO's problems.

You need to draw a very fine line between delegating and letting your team grow, and helping them make mistakes while making sure you have your fingers on the pulse of what's happening in your company. Yes, it's a fine line, and it can be a difficult one to manage.

Ultimately, it's an area that will always need your attention. Regardless of where you start, you will improve, and you will never regret the time you put into making the right decision.

Roger: A Success Story Both Ways

Although I've cautioned you about how crucial the process of hiring is, I don't want you to dwell on that to the extent that you think there are no good people out there. To emphasize that point, I'm going to conclude this chapter on a positive note by telling you about a guy named Roger. His son owned a bar in the area where I lived at the time. One night I went in for dinner, and over a few beers, the son and I talked.

Finally, he said, "Hey, my dad works at a hotel, and he's looking for another job." Then he told me his father's story.

Roger, an immigrant from India, had been working various odd jobs for twentysomething years. According to his son, Roger was constantly being mistreated, and the situation made it impossible for him to get promoted or earn a raise. This didn't make life easy for a fifty-five-year-old man with a family to provide for.

"Are you hiring right now?" the son asked me.

"Yes," I said. "Send your dad over. I'd love to meet him."

Forty-eight hours later, Roger was working for me.

Today, Roger is the most dedicated, hardworking employee I've ever had. I don't *ask* him to go on vacation. I *send* him and practically have to kick him out the door because he won't leave his job for any length of time unless I force him to. Although he's supposed to work five days a week, he is there almost every day. That's Roger.

He started with us as general manager. After that, he ended up managing four of our hotels, and then I moved him into a position of revenue manager, which is a corporate position now.

That's the only excuse he needed to blast our team with enthusiastic and encouraging social media posts 24/7, nonstop, for years. He's so passionate about the business that's he's constantly driving the team to bring in more revenue with his reminders.

"SELL SELL SELL!"

"Heads in Beds!"

"EVERY DAY has to be SOLD OUT DAY!"

His nonstop energy is infectious, and he's really one of the drivers of why we've been so successful. Yet Roger is just one example of many we've been fortunate enough to hire.

His work ethic reminds me of the one that my family exhibited when they first came to Canada. It's just the "roll up your sleeves, work your butt off, and make things happen" work ethic. When immigrants like my parents and Roger come to America, they see opportunity. Like my parents, even though he's been in this country for many years, Roger has that fresh outlook, and he spreads it throughout our company every day.

Now, finally, he's being rewarded for that outlook. He has freedom, he has employers and coworkers who appreciate and love him, and he has economic upward mobility. He is a proud, dedicated, hardworking man. As I write this book in 2020, he is making a good living and is a gift to our company. I hope he knows how much we appreciate him.

Roger just bought a beautiful home on a lake in Atlanta. Recently, I visited the home with him and took pictures of him outside it and in front of the lake. As I did so, I realized Roger—regardless of where he worked—had struggled to accomplish some symbol of financial security like this new home for his family. If the company or I played even a small part in making that happen for him, that's even more motivation for me. It helps me imagine what would be possible if we could do that for thousands of people every day. Ultimately, Roger's success is a blessing both for him and for us.

Lessons Learned

- Accountability is key. Everyone must answer to someone. The smaller the company, the more important this is.

- Continuous group chats among team members may seem strange to you, but it's really worked for our company.

- Lists help team members hold each other accountable.

- Assessments can help you decide if someone's values and priorities are a good fit for a particular position.

- Remember the three components of evaluating employees. Do they "get" the job? Do they want the job? Do they possess the capacity to do the job?

- Connect with and participate in peer groups to learn how others deal with challenges and to make those all-important connections.

- There's a reason busy, successful people make time to read. Be one of those people, starting now.

- When you delegate, know that you are dealing with both financial and emotional components.

- Strive for innovation, but never take your pulse off the business.

- Whatever you do, try to find yourself a Roger.

We all have dreams for our businesses and our futures. Have you thought about the kind of entrepreneur you want to be? Have you thought about what you want to give back? I'll share some ideas with you in the next chapter.

CHAPTER 7

THE SOCIAL ASPECT

Train people well enough so they can leave. Treat them well enough so they don't want to.

—**Richard Branson**

From that very first hotel, and even before then, I cared about people. I don't think it's incompatible to want to be successful in business and to help others. In fact, being successful in business gives you an opportunity to give back in unique ways if you look around for where the need is. For instance, tennis legend Andy Roddick could simply write checks for any cause that struck his fancy. Although he's still writing checks, he relocated back to Austin, Texas, and his nonprofit provides kids with a summer learning program, an overnight spring break camp, family nights, and many other opportunities to help children find their passions. Into his nineties, President Jimmy Carter worked for Habitat for Humanity, building homes for those who were willing to invest sweat equity to provide better lives for their families. Those who are blessed with the greatest successes have both the means and the obligation to improve life for others.

A Social Entrepreneur

Imagine your typical school day. Kids with wealthy parents have their cars and their friends. Other kids might head to the local Boys and Girls Club on their way home. Still others might have sports or clubs after school. Then there are the kids who live in hotels like the ones I own. Where do they go? Who is going to care about them? More important, how are they going to change their lives so that they don't put their own children in the same situation in which they're struggling? Before we get into that, I want to talk about my dual vision and what I'm doing about it. I'm hoping this might inspire you to think about your own vision and how you might start, right now, moving toward it.

The ultimate vision I have for our company is twofold—business and social. On the business side, my vision is to have ten thousand rooms across the United States. On the social side, the process of acquiring those ten thousand rooms will allow us to create more than two thousand jobs.

Furthermore, I want to continue to support the local nonprofits that provide school tutoring programs in the communities where our properties are located. We recently launched such a program at our Marietta location. Kids staying at the hotel currently receive free after-school tutoring.

YELLS (Youth Empowerment through Learning, Leading, and Serving), the organization we support in Marietta, has a goal of empowering young people to become active, healthy, and productive members of their communities. Founded in 2008 by high school teacher Laura Keefe in collaboration with various schools and nonprofit and community organizations, its many partners include the Marietta Police Athletic League, Marietta City Schools, Big Brothers Big Sisters, the Franklin Road Community Association—and us.

The flagship YELLS Mentoring Program matches high school "Bigs" as mentors for elementary school "Littles" and empowers them to lead large-scale service initiatives. Everything about YELLS centers on building community through service and collaboration. The result has been youth with confidence, character, and academic excellence.[9]

Laura Keefe simply saw the need inner city kids had, starting with tutoring. In Marietta, inner city kids who want tutoring can just knock on the door, and it won't cost them a dime. This program gives them a place to go after school where they can experience a sense of community as they learn with mentors who care about them. It's a great opportunity and a great way to fill that time right after school when too many kids can get into trouble.

Fortunately for us, the YELLS headquarters is just down the street from our hotel. Laura came in one day a couple of years ago and told me about the program. Since then, I'm proud to say that we've donated about $20,000 to the program. That's because I believe if we're going to give money to a cause, let's donate it to something with substance. I really believe education can solve a lot of the problems for adults—and their children—in the inner city. While sending a kid to a camp with some toys is great, it's just not enough for me. I want to see kids have the opportunity to finish high school and go to college, because that's really going to change their lives. The toys around the Christmas holidays may feel good for a day. I'm not against that, but my passion is having a long-term, sustainable influence on people. YELLS gives me that avenue.

Although I might not have called it that at the time, I felt from the day that we started the business, in the back of my mind, that I wanted to be a social entrepreneur, meaning I've always wanted the

---

9   "About YELLS," YELLS Inc., accessed August 3, 2020, https://www.yellsinc.org/about.

business that we've created to mean something more than just dollars and cents.

Earlier, I talked about Barbara, the recent widow who went from daily drinking as a resident in our first hotel to working for us as a housekeeper and ultimately moving up to a front desk manager. Stories like hers are micro-opportunities for entrepreneurs to make a difference. Then there are the macro-opportunities like what we're doing with YELLS and our own after-school program in Marietta.

So what is a social entrepreneur? It's someone like Tatsuya Nakagawa, who cofounded Castagra Products, specializing in the production of ecofriendly building materials. One of its most popular products, Ecodur, is changing the world by replacing toxic products that are commonly used in industrial facility maintenance. To date, it's approved by organizations such as BP, Shell, General Mills, Sysco, Encana, Tyson Foods, Giant Foods, Whole Foods, Columbia University—and the list just keeps on growing. The product was even voted top green invention on *Dragons' Den* and *Shark Tank*.

> **Being a social entrepreneur is as much about heart as it is about money.**

A social entrepreneur is someone like Shaun Bradley, who, after serving in the US Navy, cofounded Bradley-Morris Inc. (BMI) and became known as one of the founding fathers of the veteran recruiting industry, which has placed tens of thousands of veterans into positions in American industry—all at no cost to them. Shaun and BMI were honored at the White House as one of the top small businesses in the country. Who would've known that when BMI opened its doors in 1991, it would grow to become a multistate operation, placing over fifteen thousand veterans with annual sales eclipsing $15 million, and would become one of the largest nonfranchise staffing firms in the United States?

Being a social entrepreneur is as much about heart as it is about money. Yes, you need to have the resources to help, but just as important, you have to recognize the causes that call out to you. And, simply, you need to care.

Other Programs, Other Services: Breaking the Cycle

At one of our other hotels, we started an after-school program for the kids at our properties. As I spent more time at the properties and met the people who were living there, I couldn't ignore the fact that these kids did not choose to be in their current situations; they were just born into them. I would look at some of them and think, *Wow. You did not choose to be born into a family where your father is not there, and your mother's away trying to pay the bills, and here you are living in a hotel, and no one knows what you need.*

My bigger sympathy lies with the children because they're innocent bystanders in the whole drama of their lives. Of course, as is usually the case, the parents of those kids didn't choose either, because they're coming from backgrounds where they encountered the same challenges and situations, and now they are continuing the cycle. How do we break the cycle? I believe in education. I believe in the work we are doing with YELLS, and I believe in what we're doing with the after-school program at our other hotel.

My mentors always told me, "Find out who your customers are, and then serve them in any and every way possible." From the beginning, I asked myself, "Who is my customer?" and the answer was clear. My customer is someone one step and a few dollars away from being homeless. So how can we serve them the best way possible?

It's not just by providing them with housing. From a social perspective, their needs are so much broader than that. Yes, housing is essential, but what then? High-end hotels will offer their guests a cocktail hour. We definitely don't need that. Instead, we offer an educational hour for our customers because that is part of what they need. We want them to take advantage of some of these other opportunities the hotels offer. We want them to know that their lives matter.

> ## Ultimately, we want to be a net benefit to the local communities we serve.

My goal is to build on what we're doing now and to continue to build our social fabric as a company. Ultimately, we want to be a net benefit to the local communities we serve. We *can* choose how we work with those individuals to give them a hand up rather than a handout.

Here are ten tips on becoming a social entrepreneur:

1. What are you doing right now or what do you want to do, and who are the people you will be serving? Identify your passion.

2. What do those people need in addition to the product or service you are providing?

3. How can you provide what they need? Write out a plan.

4. What will be your first step?

5. What will be your challenges? Create a plan for how you'll deal with them.

6.   Research who has accomplished goals similar to yours.

7.   How did those people succeed as social entrepreneurs?

8.   What were their individual challenges?

9.   Investigate in depth. Did they really change lives, or did they just win awards? Find *true* role models.

10.   Identify your funding sources, and make a budget.

When I reflect on some of the stories and the background of how we've worked with our customer base to give them employment and/or educational opportunities, I think we've done well, and I'm excited about how we can do more. I don't think I could have accomplished all that I have if I didn't care about the people who live in our hotels. Even though our business has grown to cover other types of investment properties, I'm not selling widgets. Primarily, I'm selling rooms, by the night, to people who might not otherwise have a bed in which to sleep. I'm employing some people who might have once been one step away from being homeless. I never forget that. And to me, those two words, *social* and *entrepreneur,* are not exclusive. Together, they can be stronger than either one is alone.

Lessons Learned

- You can be successful in business, and you can also try to make the world—your part of it, anyway—a better place.

- Some of the most successful entrepreneurs are social entrepreneurs.

- Do some research, and discover what that term means to you.

- Find out who your customers are, and serve them in the best way possible—for them.

- If you feel good about what you're doing, you're probably doing good.

If you've read this far, I'm guessing you can relate to at least part of my message. You might even be asking yourself how you can make investments similar to mine. That's what we'll discuss in the next chapter. Although it may go against what you've assumed about investing, I intend to convince you not to overlook undervalued assets.

CHAPTER 8

BUYING UNDERVALUED ASSETS

Be fearful when others are greedy, and be greedy when others are fearful.
—Warren Buffet

Some more straightforward investments may appear to have it all: relatively high rental rates, placement in posh neighborhoods, and proximity to the finest restaurants. Those are typical qualities of the Class A/B properties that reel in an investor—maybe you—hook, line, and sinker. The sinker part can also describe the way you feel when you start trying to maintain those luxuries and hang on to the tenants who expect them.

When searching for your treasure, don't let the advertisements for high-end properties cause you to overlook a mine full of hidden gems that are not always observable at first glance. Class C properties, which you'll find in more neglected areas, can be much more lucrative, especially after you make some initial investments for refinement.

With the right guidance, focusing on Class C properties in lower-income areas is a great way for you to find your next diamond in the rough.

Find the Right Deal

Each investor needs to understand what the right deal looks like to them. Some investors may be looking for value-add opportunities, while others want to increase short-term cash flow or long-term equity. Understanding the objective will help garner your search.

Provide this information to your personal network of brokers and other real estate professionals. Leverage these business relationships to help you get more eyes searching the market. Be sure to provide them with clear parameters on the deal you are targeting.

Use online search tools such as Facebook Marketplace and LoopNet to find budget-priced properties with a lot of potential. Pay special attention to listings that have been removed. The seller may have pulled a listing after being unsuccessful and will therefore be in a suitable position to bargain.

Finally, take advantage of the research that has already been done for you. Learn where online crowdfunding and investing platforms are placing their current deals, and follow their leads. These companies need to do a lot of market research before investing in a particular area and encouraging others to invest with them.

Research the Potential for Success

Before purchasing any property, you should learn about any growth the neighborhood is expected to undergo over the next four to five years. Is there sufficient transportation to facilitate that growth? Are there schools and shopping areas nearby?

Here are a few specifics to watch out for based on property type:

- With multifamily properties and hotels, avoid the risk of vacancy by ensuring the surrounding area has a sufficient residential and tourist population.

- When buying single-family residential homes, assess the potential for mortgage helpers, such as basement suites or new additions.

- If you want to purchase abandoned spaces, you should target lower-income neighborhoods to leverage the country's Opportunity Zone program, intent on spurring economic growth in these areas.

Create a Win-Win

Once you spot your jewel, you need to acquire it. If there is room for negotiation, start preparing. Find out more about the seller's financial position and key motivations to help develop a proposal that's enticing to both of you.

The first step in creating a win-win situation is to be sure you're dealing with the right person. You'll be safest from a legal standpoint if you go through the real estate broker; however, seasoned investors, especially those with experience buying Class C properties, may find it more effective to negotiate directly with the seller.

> While doing research, prepare a strong leverage point, and stick with it during the negotiation.

The next step is to enter the negotiation armed with meaningful data. The information age has created a paradigm shift in the way negotiations are handled. Nowadays, everyone has access to the same data, evening the edge between buyer and seller. Both parties must be convinced their problem will be solved by completing the deal.

While doing research, prepare a strong leverage point, and stick with it during the negotiation. For example, ask the seller to consider how long they may need to wait until the property appreciates before they get their initial asking price, how much business they can lose in the meantime, and where the bank stands on lending to other investors who want to buy Class C properties. Use the facts to help them understand why their potential jackpot might already be sitting right in front of them, across the other side of the negotiating table.

Convert the Asset to Optimal Use

Once the asset is acquired, you have yourself a raw diamond, ready for refinement. The conversion process, however, varies for each property type.

With multifamily properties and hotels, the priority is to get rooms in service. As I shared earlier in this book, you need to immediately assess the status of the rooms, especially for potential health and safety hazards, so that you can help plan a budget and timeline for capital investments.

In single-family residential areas, it is important to maintain the trends and quality of life you've observed throughout the neighborhood. Ensure the property's interior and exterior design elements align with those undercurrents.

Abandoned spaces, such as warehouses, must be redesigned to create business revenue as soon as possible. Research what services are required by local or adjacent communities as well as the legal requirements for zoning.

I believe that the right amount of research, initial investment, and out-of-the-box thinking will allow most Class C investments to flourish, more so than their Class A/B counterparts. Following these basic guidelines will go a long way for any investor whose goal is to create passive or active rental income. And if the process of searching for and refurbishing your property becomes laborious, simply outsource these services to seasoned investors who have mastered the art of finding and refining these hidden gems to a splendor.

Lessons Learned

- Consider the benefits of Class C properties in lower-income areas.

- Take advantage of online tools to find properties.

- Get rooms in service as soon as possible in multifamily properties and hotels.

- Maintain trends and quality of life in single-family residential areas.

- Consider outsourcing to experienced investors.

But what if you're buying your very first multifamily property? We're going to talk about that next. When I bought my first multi-family project, I was willing to work hard and learn all I had to. In the next chapter, I'm going to share with you what I wish I'd known.

CHAPTER 9

HOW TO BUY YOUR FIRST MULTIFAMILY PROPERTY

If you don't own a home, buy one. If you own one home, buy another one. And if you own two homes, buy a third and lend your relatives the money to buy one.

—John Paulson

Once an investor acquires a few single-family residential properties, the management of each property can become a full-time job, with plenty of overtime. Take it from someone who's been there: running between properties to coordinate maintenance and completing administrative tasks can take its toll.

That was the situation I found myself in before relocating from Canada to Atlanta, Georgia, where I could expand my real estate portfolio to include multifamily properties. Within a few years, I was able to consolidate my assets and collect more income from each property. I was also able to drastically reduce the time I spent running between individual single-family properties.

If you find yourself in the same dilemma I was in before consolidating my assets, here are a few tips to help you navigate your options.

Explore New Horizons

When living in a city where real estate prices surpass the average income earner's capacity for buying a property, look for a new destination to call home. In many cases, you can achieve this by moving just a few hours away.

> If your goal is to expand your real estate portfolio, your primary home cannot be a vacuum for all your investing income.

If your goal is to expand your real estate portfolio, your primary home cannot be a vacuum for all your investing income. Furthermore, you should not have to wait years to save up for the initial down payment on each property. Cities like Santa Cruz, California, or Miami, Florida, although prime areas for living, would not be ideal destinations for an investor acquiring their first multifamily asset.

Target Gentrification

Buying real estate in neighborhoods that offer the best public services, facilities, and transportation will, inevitably, eat into your profit margin. Instead, target real estate in unrefined areas still undergoing gentrification, or even in a state of dilapidation, that also have a dense population. Cities like Detroit and Atlanta contain prime examples of these neighborhoods, which might even be minutes away from the downtown core. Furthermore, property prices in these areas can be as low as $10,000 to $30,000 per home.

Purchase multiple properties in order to make a sizable return that can be used toward a down payment on your first multifamily acquisition. For example, my company purchased eight single-family houses in downtown Atlanta at approximately $12,000 each in 2013. After some minor renovations and simply observing urban growth over the next five years, each house was sold for approximately $75,000 to $100,000, giving us enough cash to acquire a nearby one hundred–bedroom hotel by 2018.

How can you predict when and where rapid gentrification will take place? Fortunately, the clues are obvious.

The most important factor to consider is location, with a bull's-eye on neighborhoods that are close to the downtown core. Ensure that the surrounding area is ripe for gentrification, and be aware of all the policies and initiatives that exist to promote this growth.

Investors who can battle the disorder of these sometimes socioeconomically challenged areas, and even contribute to their refinement, could likely see sizable dividends in four to five years.

Also, check out the daily news to learn about growing or emerging manufacturing hubs in different regions around the country. These cities will develop a bustling population and labor force ready to purchase real estate and contribute to the local economy.

Redeem your 1031

Once you've found the right multifamily property to acquire, you can sell one or more single-family properties while using a tax-deferral initiative known as the 1031 exchange.

The policy allows you to defer capital gains tax that you would otherwise have to pay on a property you are selling to the property you are purchasing. Both properties, however, must be classified as investment properties. Neither can be your primary home.

You can continue to defer the capital gains tax in this manner as long as the property being sold is in the same investment category as the property being purchased. Essentially, this frees up more cash to put toward the new, more expensive property. Take some time to research the policy, because there are many rules that you will need to follow.

Adding multifamily properties to your portfolio can be an exciting milestone for any investor. If it's not done prudently, however, the investment can become your worst nightmare. Before acquiring the first multifamily asset, be sure your personal debt and primary mortgage will not eat into your investment income. If necessary, consider, as I did, relocating to an area that allows you to reach your goals much faster.

Lessons Learned

- When living in a city where real estate prices surpass the average income earner's capacity for buying a property, look for a new destination to call home.

- Target real estate in unrefined areas still undergoing gentrification, or even in a state of dilapidation, that also have a dense population.

- Learn about growing or emerging manufacturing hubs in different regions around the country.

- Explore deferring capital gains tax.

So if you're thinking multifamily, let's keep thinking outside the box. In the next chapter, I'm going to share with you an investment opportunity we wouldn't have considered ten years ago, and that's because it didn't exist.

CHAPTER 10

AIRBNB—HOW TO GET STARTED

Real estate cannot be lost or stolen, nor can it be carried away.
Purchased with common sense, paid for in full, and managed with
reasonable care, it is about the safest investment in the world.

—Franklin Delano Roosevelt

Airbnb first grabbed my attention during the 2010 Vancouver Winter Olympics. My two-bedroom condo, which I usually rented out for $1,200 per month, suddenly earned me more than $400 per night. If I rented it only one week a month, I would already earn more than double what I had before. While the world watched athletes tackle the ski slopes, I stared wide eyed at the upward slope of my returns.

But it doesn't take the Olympics to turn a handsome profit through Airbnb. Position yourself right, and you will find your properties competing in the same market as high-end local hotels.

To capitalize on the vacation rental market back in the day, you had to optimize your home location and perform all your own

> Now anyone with a spare bedroom, investment house, or in-law suite can make a decent profit from local tourism.

marketing across multiple platforms just to get your space noticed by prospective vacationers. Airbnb did away with that model. Now anyone with a spare bedroom, investment house, or in-law suite can make a decent profit from local tourism.

Here are some strategies for getting started or scaling your Airbnb properties to achieve maximum profits.

Run the Numbers to See If Short Term Is for You

Give your property a test run. I brought what I learned in Vancouver back to Atlanta. With the first vacation rental property we bought in the Edgewood neighborhood of Atlanta, we averaged about 70 percent occupancy rate and raked in between $200 and $400 per night, depending on the property. I paid down my mortgages and began scaling my business.

You're Now in the Vacation Rental Business—So Think Like a Hotel

Hotels win occupancy through privacy and by fulfilling guests' expectations of amenities that reflect the comforts of home. You'll do best to follow their example.

Consider the needs of your clients before they do: cutlery, an extra toothbrush, soft towels, an ironing board, bath mats, cooking essentials, a coffee setup. Help guests feel comfortable.

Remember to consider safety: first aid kit, fire extinguisher, and functioning smoke detectors. Give clear instructions for adjusting the AC and parking. No one wants to worry about getting towed on their vacation.

Learn to answer the questions before they're asked. That will help you automate the short-term rental process.

Optimize Design to Cater to Vacationers

Give people an experience of the city they won't forget.

Add some art that is reflective of the city guests are visiting. If your property is in Detroit, consider a "Detroit Hustles Harder" flag or some local graphic design for the walls. In Colorado, try decorating with some national parks posters. You can look for a map of your city on Etsy and frame it as the centerpiece of the living room or bedroom of your rental.

If you have a blank slate, and you don't know where to get started, then don't waste your time. Hire professional interior designers to get the job done right.

In Airbnb, as in Everything, Lean into Your Strengths

Plan to outsource. If you think repairs may look shoddy if you do them yourself, don't sacrifice the character of your space to save a few hundred dollars.

If your real estate portfolio boasts more than a few properties, don't worry about the nitty-gritty. Consider the Pareto principle—the 80/20 rule—of life optimization. As a theory, the Pareto principle is a way of looking at economics. In practice, it is an efficiency scheme that instructs you to perform the 20 percent of work that produces 80 percent of the results. Outsource or eliminate the excess 80 percent. The same rule is practical in the short-term rental market.

Automation Means Saying Goodbye to Common Rental Headaches

Airbnb does more than provide homeowners with a platform for marketing their rental spaces. It takes over some of the biggest headaches associated with long-term rentals.

With long-term renters, if it's a bad fit, you have to go through the eviction process to get them out. Short-term rentals take the headache out of getting rent from your tenants in the traditional way. With vacation rentals, you receive money seamlessly through the platform.

In addition to simplifying the exchange of money, the review system in Airbnb lets you and your guests read actual feedback to learn more about each other. Members tend to understand that reviews are currency in the sharing economy, so they're less likely to trash a place or do any harm. This works in everyone's favor.

Passive versus Active Rental Oversight: The Choice Is Yours

Some investors believe it is better to lease properties the traditional way because they value passive over active income. But Airbnb is still on the table if your goal is passive income. Buy a lockbox so guests can check in at their convenience. Hire a property manager to clean each house or room after the latest guest has checked out. This doesn't have to be costly. More often than not, preparing a home for a new guest is simple.

Short-term rentals equate to higher daily earnings, making it easy to afford the extra cost of a property manager. And since they need to stop by only after someone has stayed, there's no chance of losing money when your house hits a seasonal dry spell.

Market to Your Dream Client

Whether you lease your home for years, months, or nights at a time, real estate investment is about business ownership. There are diverse demographics out there, each willing to pay vastly different prices for a place to stay. Take practical steps to appeal to higher-paying guests, and charge the rates that they expect for a more luxurious experience.

In this market, there will always be a race to the bottom for pricing. Catch the attention of vacationers willing to pay higher prices to stay in your home. These people tend to treat your property more respectfully than those who will try to nickel-and-dime you over everything.

Lessons Learned

- Position yourself right, and you will find your properties competing in the same market as high-end local hotels.

- Give your property a test run.

- Consider the needs of your clients before they do.

- Give people an experience of the city they won't forget.

- Know that Airbnb takes over some of the biggest headaches associated with long-term rentals.

As you can see, investing from the ground up can take on many different forms. As our business grew, we began to see not only that vacation rentals were a good addition to our own portfolio, but that they might be for other investors as well.

In the next chapter, I'm going to talk about asset diversification. I'll also share with you my 60/20/20 rule.

CHAPTER 11

ASSET DIVERSIFICATION

Buy real estate in areas where the path exists, and buy more real estate where there is no path but you can create your own.

—David Waronker

I've always been a strong believer in diversification or, in other words, not putting all our eggs in one basket. Typically, when we want to learn about how to diversify our assets, the information provided through general research is about how to diversify your overall portfolio, one that includes public investments, such as stocks and bonds, as well as private investments, such as private equity funds and real estate.

The problem with public markets, however, is that they're shrinking. The number of IPOs has dropped by 50 percent over the last twenty years. Industries such as the airlines, banking, and social media are dominated by just a few major players.[10] Although I still

---

10   Randy Brown, "Shrinking U.S. Public Market Is Boosting Corporate Profits," *Forbes*, February 25, 2020, https://www.forbes.com/sites/randy-brown/2020/02/25/shrinking-us-public-market-is-boosting-corporate-profits/#33b7ec3514e2.

invest in the public market, I prefer to keep my overall allocation to a minimum.

I've learned that, in the long term, we get a bigger bang for our buck in the private market. And so, for this chapter, let's focus solely on how to diversify within it or, more specifically, within your real estate portfolio.

My allocation approach is simple. I call it the 60/20/20 rule.

1. 60 Percent for Multiresidential Properties

The ideal scenario for any real estate investor is, at a minimum, doubling their cash flow from the same square footage they receive with a single-family property. The security and consistency of such an investment also makes up for the volatility of our investments in other markets or asset classes. That's why I park the majority of our firm's funds in this piece of the pie. During times like these, while inflation is rising and fewer people can afford luxury homes, there will always be a growing demand for affordable living space.

When purchasing a multifamily property, remember the initial cost must be low enough to ensure that property is cash flowing positive very soon after the purchase.

This doesn't mean, however, that you should focus solely on turnkey investments. As we've discussed throughout this book, older buildings in low-income areas, for example, may require an additional investment to bring their living standards up to code. The revenue gained from steady, long-term renters will likely reward that investment with sizable dividends shortly thereafter.

2. 20 Percent for Vacation Rentals

Although holiday planning is not top of mind for everyone right now because of COVID-19, it's important to remember we're in a situation that will not last forever. Just as crude oil prices have dropped, their resurgence is as inevitable as our driving cars to and from work again. In a similar vein, whether it's for family, business, or personal reasons, we'll all need to travel abroad and find accommodation again.

Vacation rentals are another great way to gain more income from the same square footage you would receive after purchasing a single-family property.

While managing our firm's portfolio of vacation rentals, I've seen how easily hosts can make three times more on short-term rentals than they would make with long-term rentals in the same space. When this rental is located near a popular event space, such as an arena for hockey games or an outdoor space that hosts annual festivals, profits can soar even higher, up to ten times as much.

3. 20 Percent for Private Equity Real Estate Funds

Private equity or real estate firms, such as SGH, often take on the roles of fund and property managers. Once they find contributors for a blind pool fund, also known as a blank-check offering, investors could be rewarded with a significant amount of passive income.

When funds include investments on multifamily properties, it's a huge benefit to contributors because much of the legwork is done for them. In our case, for example, all the staffing, security, insurance, ongoing maintenance, marketing, accounting, and legal services, to name a few, are outsourced.

The 60/20/20 rule works best for seasoned real estate investors who enjoy taking an active role in the management of their properties, because it gives them a balance between earning active and passive income. Those who prefer earning more passive income, and who have found a private equity firm with a great track record they can trust, should consider increasing this piece of the pie.

If you're an avid investor in the public markets, I still recommend increasing your investments in private equity funds in addition to multiresidential properties. Vacation rentals, on the other hand, can be subject to volatility during times like these, while you may be getting enough instability in the public markets.

Although it's hard to predict where public markets will go in the next twenty to thirty years, it's never a complete waste of time to invest in stocks and bonds, especially for those who study this market on a regular basis.

I recommend keeping the majority of your funds planted in real estate. It's bound to be stable as long as the world's supply of land is diminishing and people need homes to live in.

Lessons Learned

- My 60/20/20 rule will allow you to diversify: 60 percent for multiresidential properties, 20 percent for vacation rentals, and 20 percent for private equity funds.

- This approach provides you with a balance between earning active and passive income.

- I still believe you should keep most of your money in real estate.

To invest in any of the opportunities I've presented here, you need to raise capital. I'd like to add just one word to that. You need to raise capital responsibly. We're going to address that next.

CHAPTER 12

RAISING CAPITAL RESPONSIBLY

Learn to raise capital by any means necessary. That's your primary job as an entrepreneur. You must continually raise capital from family and friends, banks, suppliers, customers, and investors.

—Richard Branson

As investors, when we hear about self-made millionaires making it all on their own, it's important that we understand the extent of the term *self-made*. Building wealth on a million- or billion-dollar scale is typically not something any one person can accomplish alone.

Although independence is always ideal, I've learned these ventures won't always work when we try to do them solo, saving up for one large down payment at a time. We need to use other people's money (OPM) and become comfortable with walking away from a portion of the profit.

Banks have made an industry out of using OPM to raise capital, lend money, and reinvest. As sophisticated investors who have good performance records, we need to look beyond a bank's ability to lend to us and, instead, learn from their long history of how to raise capital responsibly.

Starting a Private Equity Real Estate Fund

Put simply, banks first started raising capital by reaching out to a pool of investors and enticing them to trust the bank with their funds to raise more money. In return, investors could look forward to the safekeeping of their cash and interest payments.

Similarly, investors can take on the role of fund managers once they find contributors for a blind pool fund, also known as a blank-check offering.

Real estate investment funds are like mutual funds, except the majority of the inventory is made up of commercial and residential properties. These funds gain value through appreciation, property improvements, and rental income. Customers who buy shares would receive the same portfolio management support they would receive with any other mutual fund.

As their fund manager, you have the flexibility to use their investment to raise more capital as you see fit, as long as you fulfill the obligations of your agreement with them. Typically, this obligation includes making regular interest payments and sending out a quarterly report or facilitating regular conference calls to provide a breakdown of investment activity.

To create the fund structure, hire an attorney who specializes in asset management and investment funds. These are the experts who can ensure your fund complies with all the necessary security regulations.

Seller Financing

Some investors may not have the performance record or experience that fund contributors want to see before entrusting them with managing their hard-earned dollars. That's when investors need to narrow down to fewer candidates.

With seller financing, for example, when you're buying real estate already owned outright by the seller, you only need to earn one person's trust—the seller's.

Sellers are attracted to this type of financing because they can earn a higher sale price for their home without having to fork out any capital of their own. The terms of the arrangement are usually laid out in a promissory note that, in exchange for a transfer of ownership, allows the buyer to make regular payments toward the loan until they can fully pay it off with a larger lump-sum amount.

Even when the seller decides to increase the sales price, the buyer still benefits from fewer overhead costs compared to what they would be charged by a bank for underwriting, appraisals, or legal clearing of an application. The buyer is also granted an opportunity they otherwise may not have had, albeit at a higher cost.

Sellers should consult a real estate lawyer to ensure they are protected from fraud and they hold the first lien on the asset.

Joint Ventures

The fewer people you need to help you raise capital, the easier it is to do. What makes it even easier is a strong track record in real estate investing with outstanding returns or equity ownership as solid proof.

Once you have enough experience and evidence of your success, you can raise capital through joint ventures. In my experience, this has been the easiest and most effective way to build wealth for each partner.

Partners like this setup because they have more control over how the investment is managed and, if they choose, can actively take part in investment activities. Alternatively, they can be silent partners and still be shareholders with a stake in ownership.

Regardless of which channel one chooses to raise OPM, the pitfalls to success remain the same. Ensure every investor is on the same page and that each other's objectives are clearly communicated from the beginning. Try to bring different areas and levels of expertise to the venture; however, avoid bringing completely different leadership styles together, because doing so can easily result in little or no cooperation.

Right about now, you might be wondering how you can leverage OPM if you don't have the track record you need to showcase your potential. If you don't have it, build it. Once you do have success raising OPM, however, the benefits are boundless. You can grow your portfolio exponentially in a way you would never be able to do by working a nine-to-five job.

> Avoid bringing completely different leadership styles together, because doing so can easily result in little or no cooperation.

Once you can prove your ability to manage OPM and provide the returns your partners require, you can also charge the appropriate fees. When OPM is raised the right way, avoiding common pitfalls and using the correct legal framework, it becomes a win-win for everyone who takes part in the venture.

Lessons Learned

- Building wealth on a million- or billion-dollar scale is typically not something any one person can accomplish alone.

- Investors can take on the role of fund managers once they find contributors for a blind pool fund, also known as a blank-check offering.

- With seller financing, you need the trust of only one other person—the seller's.

- The fewer people you need to raise capital, the easier it is to do.

- Make sure all investors are on the same page.

- Clearly communicate your objectives from the start—and listen to theirs.

- Prove your ability to manage OPM, and then go for it.

"If I only knew then what I know now." That's something we all feel from time to time, yet the axiom that there's no substitute for experience is truly the case. In the next chapter, I'm going to share with you some of what I've learned about investing.

CHAPTER 13

INVESTMENT LESSONS

Real estate investing, even on a very small scale, remains a tried and true means of building an individual's cash flow and wealth.

—**Robert Kiyosaki**

When I look back over this amazing journey of ours—my family's, my employees', and mine—I believe that the right people and the way we treated those people got us where we are today. I'm grateful to many, starting with my uncle, who, when we had that conversation on our first night in our first hotel, said essentially, "Look, Ali. You know you can sell these rooms for $25 a night, and we could fill up overnight. Instead of trying to go for high rent, sell your rooms on volume."

Those were the magic words, and that was the impetus for me. Maybe it was because I had all the exuberance and optimism that come with youth. Maybe it's because I knew my uncle was a very wise man. Maybe I just heard the ring of truth in his voice. I remember thinking, *Yeah. Why can't we do that?*

I've spoken to a lot of hotel owners, and let me tell you, if I said to them what my uncle said to me, they would look at me as if I were completely out of my mind. They'd say things like, "Well, you're devaluing our asset. You're devaluing the business model by doing that." But I felt then what I know now. My uncle just had such a creative and brilliant way of looking at how to start earning money from the start.

"At the end of the day, if that room remains empty tonight, you're going to make $0, so why don't you at least get $25?"

That made sense to me because it was very practical, very realistic. And I think that birthed the business model that was also as pragmatic as it was far thinking. That business model continues to work for our investors today.

As I told you in the first chapter, I started out as a seventeen-year-old kid who wanted a cool car. I went from that dashed and, yes, foolish dream to becoming the owner of a condominium. (Thanks, Mom.) Along the way between there and where I am now, I've learned a great deal. The first lesson is this:

Be Creative

Experts can talk to you all day about price-to-rent ratio, capitalization rate, cash flow, and gross rental yield. Yet those stats don't even scratch the surface when it comes to the potential return on investment.

It doesn't matter if you're looking at a condo or a hotel worth millions of dollars. When you look at a piece of real estate, you have to be creative and flexible in your thinking. If you are a microinvestor, and you want to buy your very first condo, you might be disappointed when you realize the condo you can afford will rent only $700 a month. That's when you get creative. How many bedrooms in that condo? Two! Why, then, don't you rent it out by the room for $400 or $500 a month? All of a sudden, you have a cash flow of $800 or $1,000 a month instead of the smaller amount you would have received for renting out the whole thing. That's thinking creatively!

At one time, we bought nine properties at $12,000 to $13,000 each. My initial plan was to renovate them, which I did, and then to wait while gentrification helped the properties increase in value. Then something amazing happened. At first what happened appeared to be a negative. During the process of my renovating the houses in those neighborhoods, people started breaking into them and stealing all the construction supplies. It was *Groundhog Day* from day one. When the contractors went home for the night, they'd leave all their tools and supplies in there, and someone would break into the house and steal all the materials, and we would have to start from ground zero every day.

Okay, I thought. *This is not working.* There was no way I could watch over this place at night, and all my employees had plenty to do. Then I remembered Nate, one of the guys who was staying with us at the hotel. He had started helping us out by picking up garbage and performing other small tasks. Furthermore, he was trustworthy and willing to work.

One day, I asked him, "Nate, would you mind staying at this house for the night? I'll pay you to stay there, monitor to make sure nothing happens there, and be a watchful eye."

"Sure," he said.

Instead of his room at the hotel, Nate had an entire house, and he was getting paid to watch over it. That made him happy. I knew I could depend on him to keep people from stealing from us, and that made me happy.

As the renovations were completed, Nate stayed there every night. Finally he came to me.

"You know, I've really gotten used to that house," he told me. "I like it. Would you mind if I rented it from you? I could pay you $500 a month."

Tempting as that offer was, I understood the downside all too well.

"Look, Nate, you're a good guy," I said. "But I don't want to have to chase you around for $500 a month in case you don't pay your rent. Let's not go in that direction, because it's going to create nothing but problems for both of us."

"No," he insisted. "I already figured it out. You can take it out of my paycheck. Every two weeks, take out 250 bucks from my paycheck, and that way I don't have to think about it, and you can get your rent."

I could hardly believe what a perfect solution he had presented me with. Instead of my paying him to watch the house, he would pay me so that he could live there. The benefit to him was clear as well.

"Nate, that's a great idea," I told him. "Let's try it."

Our arrangement worked so well that he ended up living there for about three years, and I now had a plan to protect my new investments as well as provide housing for some of my staff members. Right away, I started placing my employees—housekeepers and maintenance people—in the company's homes. As I mentioned earlier, many of these people were at one time residents in our hotels. Now they had an opportunity for upward mobility. I didn't want to rent to strangers in these areas that were still developing, but I trusted and knew my people. It was a win-win situation because they got houses, I got $500 for rent from them each month, and that money came straight out of their paychecks. It was a symbiotic partnership.

At some point, I realized that our employees had literally created a neighborhood, a community, in downtown Atlanta, living in those houses we owned. It's the same thing that I had watched happening at the hotels.

Of course, this stable sense of community no doubt hastened with gentrification, and the property values in that neighborhood began increasing. My goal was to keep holding on to those houses and let the rent come in. It was a nice, easy investment for us. We had purchased each house for about $13,000, and after putting in the money to renovate each one, we were in at around $30,000. With the approximately $6,000 a year rent I was bringing in on each one, we were realizing almost 25 percent to 30 percent return. As far as I was concerned, I would be happy to hold on to the houses for the next twenty to twenty-five years.

But turnover is part of life, and employees started to transition out of the company, taking other jobs and moving out of the houses. I was having to find new tenants, and as the managerial duties became more intensive, I considered my options. One day, I went on Zillow and started checking the values of each of the ten houses. I put in the first address and was surprised to see a figure of $150,000. The next house was $80,000, and the third house was $70,000. Could that be possible? Gentrification had started, and the soaring real estate prices were reflecting that.

I took out my calculator and added the equity that was in all the eight houses we purchased in downtown Altanta back in 2013, and it came close to $1 million. *Well, okay*, I thought. We have ten homes that we're balancing collecting rent from against maintenance and other issues. Why don't we sell all of them, take those profits, and buy a hotel? So now we would have one hundred rooms. We will have increased our portfolio, but all the rooms would be under one roof, so it would be a lot easier to manage the property. Furthermore, at the same time, we could offer affordable accommodations and still provide a service for the community.

That's what we did. We cashed out, and then we used almost all those funds to purchase another hotel.

That situation was somewhat exceptional because the value of our homes increased so rapidly. Fortunately, however, in any real estate market where the population is increasing, the value of your real estate over time is still going to go up significantly.

Figure Out the *How I Can,* Not the *Why I Can't*

Okay, tell me the truth here. What was the first thing that popped in your mind when I suggested renting out your condo to two tenants instead of one? Did you say, "Won't that be too hard?" Or, "So, now I'm going to have to deal with two tenants?" Or, "What if they don't get along?"

I ask you that because many times that's the response I get when I offer advice to entrepreneurs. When you get creative, you may need to work a little harder, but you can also make more money if you're willing to roll up your sleeves and handle the situation. Not much in life is easy. Just figure it out. Talk to your tenants—preferably before they move in. Sit down with them, and explain it's their obligation to get along. Put that in writing. Help them set up some ground rules, come in and pick up your rent every month, and manage that property accordingly.

And then buy your next condo.

Know that a great opportunity is going to come with a lot of hard work. Yes, it's going to require you to sweat a little. Take a towel, wipe off the sweat, and get going.

Don't be one of those people who makes excuses for why they can't be successful. Remember this. There are a million more people out there a billion times smarter than I am, and they could do whatever I've been able to do a lot of times over. Instead, they're making excuses.

I'm the first to point out that I have been richly blessed with the perfect storm of opportunities. I've been blessed with investments, family, incredible support from a very young age—but at the end of the day, those blessings don't mean much if you don't put your feet on the ground and move forward.

Some people switch around that equation. They say, "Well, if only I had those blessings, then I could …"

No! Instead, if you start moving forward and start pushing yourself, those blessings will find *you*. Maybe that's just because God doesn't want to waste those blessings. Figure a way to get your feet on the ground and move forward, and the universe will come to you.

When I tell people that, many just roll their eyes, but that approach to life has been one of my major life lessons. Don't cry about what you have not been given. If you are proactive, not passive—if you take your first couple of steps, then the universe—God—will meet you halfway.

Eliminate the Legwork—Most of It

You will reduce a great deal of stress if you are able to eliminate unnecessary legwork. Digital tools are invaluable for those of us who invest in real estate. We—that means you and me and others like us—no longer have to restrict our inventory to buy and hold deals. We can invest in overseas vacation homes for premium rents or fixer-upper homes in other states. Here are some ways you can make the most of these tools.

Virtual marketplaces like Zillow or their overseas equivalents like Zoopla provide every real estate owner, buyer, or renter with anything they need to know. Mortgage applications for preapproval, mortgage calculators, price and permit history, neighborhood statistics, running costs, and local school information are all there within each listing.

Click through the picture and video galleries to get a good look at exterior and interior features—or use other tools such as Google

Maps to check out the exterior and surrounding areas. You can also use a video chat to do a walk-through of the property.

Most real estate agents have a social media presence and will likely take advantage of mobile apps such as Instagram and Facebook Marketplace to advertise their listings. They can also auction their listings on eBay or list them on Craigslist.

Regardless of the tools you employ, be sure not to waste time on investments that produce little or no cash flow. Use the simple, universal formula of income being greater than expenses to determine whether the investment is affordable for you. For example, if you are paying a mortgage of $1,200 a month while renting out your house at $1,500, you are earning a $300 surplus monthly that you can use toward other expenses.

Although tools like Trulia or Zillow cover a lot of ground— literally—we cannot rely on them alone for everything we need, such as the rate of income tax in a particular state or country. We must do our due diligence when it comes to researching any investment property.

Finally, while Google serves as a great makeshift adviser, it is not a substitute for the army of experts that every investor needs in order to acquire and then manage a property. Use social networks like LinkedIn to recruit your team of professionals in international real estate, lending, property management, accounting, and governance. If you can find someone who can get the job done at least 70 to 80 percent as well as you can, hand it over to them.

After you've identified a potential property, I still suggest going on site, viewing the property, and having a discussion with the owner or agent when possible. Investing in a property is a huge commitment, and there is always the risk of regret attached. In-person viewing and interaction will hold their value in mitigating that risk and helping you weigh what to do next. Luckily, our twenty-first-century digital approach can eliminate 90 percent of the legwork required to get you to that point.

Take the Long-Term View

The first thing you have to realize as an investor is that life is long, and business life is especially long. Obviously, none of us knows what the future holds, but I'm speaking from an entrepreneurial perspective. Many times, the people I advise say something like this: "Yeah, what you're doing is great. I only wish I had invested twenty years ago. What's the point now?"

The point is that, even amid a pandemic, life expectancy is a lot longer nowadays, and tremendous opportunity exists to invest in and prosper from purchasing properties.

> Overall, the longer that you can hold an asset, the higher likelihood of success you're going to have.

When you're investing in real estate, take that long-term view. Understand that you're looking at a five- to ten-year cycle before you can realize any sort of real value and benefit.

Overall, the longer that you can hold an asset, the higher likelihood of success you're going to have. Try for a minimum of three years. However, if you can hold on to the property for twenty years, you'll see a lot more benefits because those returns compound more aggressively over the years.

This is similar to the compound interest aspect of stock investing. Think ahead twenty-five years from now, and the odds are that asset is going to be worth a lot more money than it was when you purchased it. Your initial goal when you jump in should be the long-term one.

You want a property that will provide you with both cash flow and appreciation.

A five- to ten-year cycle is fine, and the longer you can hold that asset, the higher the likelihood of success you're going to experience.

Too many people just don't have the vision. But you can have the vision if you do what I've just outlined:

- Be creative

- Figure out how you can (instead of why you can't)

- Take the long-term view

When you develop an understanding of real estate cycles, you'll learn how to look to the future instead of worrying about the present. You aren't going to sell this property tomorrow. You are going to develop it. The first thing a novice investor will say is, "Well, that's a bad area. I don't know if I want to invest in an area like that."

The reality is that the area you're judging on its current condition is where you'll be getting the best return in the future. You're going to buy it at the best price. Hopefully, you're going to maintain it, establish a cash flow, and in the future—without taking too many losses in the interim—be able to sell it for the best price. Sometimes you can sell sooner.

A Limited Supply of Land

There will be gyrations such as what's taking place in Vancouver as I write this book. In March 2019, for example, the housing market there crashed, with sales falling to their lowest levels since 1986. Only 1,727 homes changed hands in Greater Vancouver in March, down 31.4 percent from the same month a year earlier, the Real Estate Board of Greater Vancouver reported. Prices for all housing types are falling, and the benchmark price of a detached home was down 10.5 percent in a year. Condo prices are down 5.9 percent.[11]

However, as long as the population in Vancouver is steadily increasing, the prices are always going to catch back up and ultimately spike again. The location is desirable, and people want to live there because it has a lot of unique characteristics that drive population in that direction. Additionally, not only do you have a population that wants to live there and that is migrating there, but there is a limited supply of land in habitable areas. This is extremely important, and it's a far different situation than what we experience in Atlanta, where there is a great deal of available land and the weather is moderate.

In Vancouver, you can't just go out a few miles and buy up more property. Like markets such as New York and Hong Kong, you have very limited space. But you also have high demand. The fact that so many people want to live there will drive up real estate prices in the long term. Even today, Vancouver home prices are on the rise, despite a pandemic.[12]

One important fact I've learned on this journey is that every real estate market has unique advantages to it. Even though we don't have a small amount of land that drives prices up in Atlanta, there is opportunity to increase cash flow because you can acquire property now for a lot cheaper than other places. As a result, you'll be paying a lot less on your mortgage than the cash flow that you're taking in for rent.

---

11   Canadian Press, "Home Prices Drop by a Third in Vancouver—Where the Average Price Is Still over a Million," *Financial Post*, March 4, 2019, https://financialpost.com/real-estate/vancouver-home-sales-sluggish-in-february-as-prices-continue-to-fall.

12   Kenneth Chan, "BC Home Prices to Increase by 7.7% by End of 2020 amidst Strong Recovery," Daily Hive, August 26, 2020, https://dailyhive.com/vancouver/vancouver-real-estate-market-forecast-2020-bc.

Lessons Learned

- When you search for a piece of real estate, be creative and flexible in your approach. How can you make the best use of it?

- The longer you can hold an asset, the higher the likelihood of success you can experience.

LOOKING FOR AN INVESTMENT PROPERTY?

Long ago, Ben Graham taught me that "price is what you pay; value is what you get." Whether we're talking about socks or stocks, I like buying quality merchandise when it is marked down.

—Warren Buffett

If this ground-up story of ours intrigues you, consider joining us and being part of Stablegold. Our company's innovative investment approach will take the real estate investing headaches out of your hands while providing you excellent returns. Our core focus with our investment partners is simple.

We find properties in need of managerial overhaul and physical renovations. Then we implement our proven process for turning our assets into cash flow machines. Ultimately, we provide excellent and consistent returns to our investor partners.

Stablegold invests in a wide array of real estate assets. From extended-stay hotels and quaint bed-and-breakfasts to event facilities and vacation home rentals, we have diversified our portfolio to ensure maximum returns while minimizing risk for our partners.

ABOUT THE AUTHOR

Ali Jamal went from earning minimum wage to owning and operating a real estate investment firm with 1,500 rental units that generate millions in sales annually.

Little did he know when he was only nineteen, and his mother insisted that Ali invest in his first condominium instead of buying the fancy sports car he was eyeing, that he was taking the first step of an exciting, challenging, ultimately fulfilling journey. A few years later, with family members who believed in him as investors, Ali bought his first hotel and, through a lot of work, transformed it into a residence for low- and no-income individuals.

Other hotels and more hard work followed. As he acquired these assets, his company, Stablegold Hospitality, established the Economy Hotel brand and, in doing so, pioneered a new business brand for the hospitality industry. As he better understood his client base, Ali was able to transform his purchases into fully functional residential units for hundreds who might otherwise be homeless.

Not yet forty, he has acquired a real estate portfolio with 1,500 rental units out of real estate that was once considered uninhabitable. Driving this success was his intention to not only serve the local community by saving and repurposing buildings that might well remain vacant, but also to provide housing for those who desperately need it. Of his approximately one hundred employees, some—including several managers—began as residents in one of his facilities.

Further extending efforts to serve his client base, Ali has partnered with YELLS, a local nonprofit, to offer a free biweekly after-school program to both young hotel residents and all local young people who wish to improve their core competencies such as math, science, and history. As a board member of another nonprofit, Shelters to Shutters, Ali is involved with helping to provide participants of the program, who are situationally homeless, with employment and accommodation. Throughout the year, he encourages all Economy Hotel locations to donate hotel space to local churches and community organizations for food and clothing drives as well as gift giveaways.

Today, Ali's company offers investment opportunities to those seeking excellent and consistent returns on a variety of real estate assets, including extended-stay hotels, event facilities, and vacation home rentals.

In 2019, Stablegold Hospitality was named one of Atlanta Inno's 50 on Fire—"people and companies with new funding, recent product launches, hot hires and innovative approaches to solving problems." It also won the DeKalb County Business of the Year APEX Award, presented by the DeKalb Chamber of Commerce.

In 2020, the company was recognized as a Top 25 Small Business of the Year by the Cobb Chamber of Commerce. In a separate award category, the Chamber also recognized CEO Ali Jamal as nominee for the 2020 Next Generation Award.

Most recently, he was nominated as one of the top fifteen finalists for the Emerging Entrepreneur Award presented by the Gwinnett Chamber of Commerce.